Mel Bay Presents

A Guide to Non-Jazz Improvisation

By Dick Weissman & Dan Fox

Piano Edition

CD contents

1	Basic Melody-Grace Notes	13	American Folk
2	Neighbor Notes & Passing Tones	14	Latin American & Caribbean
3	Major Scales & key of G	15	Ragtime
4	Minor Scales	16	Gospel
5	Modes-Ionian, dorian, phyrgian	17	Blues
6	Modes lydian, mixolydian, aeolian	18	Rock and Roll
7	Speciatlty Scales	19	Odd Meters
8	Adding notes to a melody	20	International
9	Chords	21	Cajun
10	Country & Western	22	Bossa Nova
11	Bluegrass	23	New Age
12	Irish		

1 2 3 4 5 6 7 8 9 0

Visit us on the Web at www.melbay.com — E-mail us at email@melbay.com

Table of Contents

Foreword

The piano and its modern descendants, electronic keyboards, are by far the most versatile musical instruments known. Although there are thousands of talented players out there, virtually all of them are taught to play from written music. The number of books that teach how to improvise are few, and most of those deal only with jazz improvisation.

This book is about non-jazz improvisation... everything from putting a few decorative touches on a pre-existing melody to a free fantasy that uses the melody and chord progression as a springboard for the player's creativity.

If you haven't improvised before, you can use this book as a road map to coming up with new and inventive solos. If you're used to improvising but don't know how you're doing it, or wish you could do better, this book will help you on your way. In Part 1 you'll learn the basic techniques of improvising; embellishments, passing tones, major and minor scales, modes, hexachords, pentatonic scales, tetrachords, adding harmony notes to a melody, drones, and chords.

In Part 2, you'll learn great tunes and how to play variations on them. Various styles are discussed and illustrated such as Country and Western, Bluegrass, Irish (Celtic), American Folk, Ragtime, Gospel, Blues, New Age and especially Latin-American including bossa nova. In the next section you'll learn about odd meters and exotic scales. The final page lists some recommended books and recordings.

It's our hope that this book will provide you with fertile ideas that will free you from the straitjacket of the written note or a particular style. There's a great deal of wonderful music out there, and learning to play as much of it as you can is a worthy and attainable goal.

Dan Fox and Dick Weissman

What You Should Know Before Starting This Book

We assume that you have studied the piano for a while and know how to play all the natural (white key) notes as well as the sharps and flats. You should also be able to play the basic rhythms in 4/4, 3/4, 2/4, 6/8 and cut time: whole notes, half notes, quarter notes, eighth notes and their equivalent rests plus dotted half and quarter notes.

Optional but highly recommended

All of us have a tendency to play faster when the music is easy and slower when it's more difficult. In order to combat this tendency and keep a steady beat, we highly recommend using a metronome. This device produces a steady stream of clicks as slow as 40 beats and as fast as 208 beats per minute. Modern metronomes are electronic* and are very reasonable in cost; a reliable one can be purchased for as little as $20.00. Many models can be set to any meter (2/4, 3/4, 4/4 etc.), marking the first beat of each measure with a loud click. Some models also produce the note A=440 which is a great help in checking if your piano is at the proper pitch. Most of the pieces in this book have a marking such as MM=80. This means that your goal is to play the piece at 80 beats per minute.

*Old-fashioned metronomes were mechanical and worked on the pendulum principle. We don't recommend them because **a)** they have to be rewound fairly often, **b)** unless they are placed on a perfectly level surface, the beats will be unequal and **c)** they cannot be set to an exact number of beats per minute, so it's more difficult to measure your progress.

Part 1—Techniques of Improvisation

What is improvisation?
Improvisation means anything from adding a few decorative touches to an existing melody to completely free improvisation that has no rules or guidelines and relies totally on the player's instinct.

What's so good about improvising?
Improvisation is a way to express your own musical personality and feelings instead of playing someone else's ideas.

How do I get started?
Learn the very simple melody below. Make sure you can play it perfectly at a moderate walking tempo of about MM=72 to MM=80. Once you have done this, study the next few pages and we'll show you different ways of improvising around the melody.

Track 1

Basic Melody

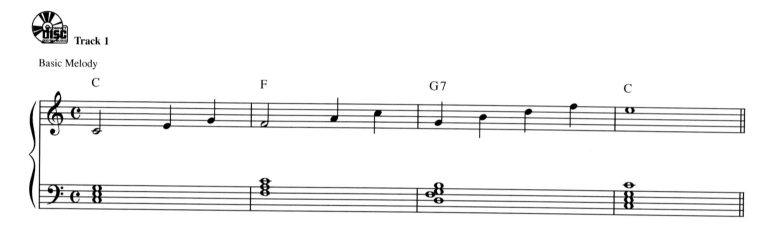

Notice that

- The tune is rhythmically very simple, using only whole notes, half notes, and quarter notes.

- Symbols for the accompanying chords are placed above the melody. These can be played on any chordal instrument such as guitar or keyboard, or, listen to the tracks on the CD that accompanies this book. **All the notes in the melody belong to these accompanying chords.** The spelling of the basic chords is as follows: C=C E G; F=F A C; G7=G B D F. Track no. 1 on the accompanying CD plays these chords so that you can hear the result of the first group of improvisations.

What's a grace note?
A grace note is a very fast note inserted before the melody note.

What does a grace note look like?
A grace note is a smaller sized note which usually takes the form of an 8th note with a diagonal line through the stem (♪).

About intervals
In this book we'll often refer to intervals. In music, an interval is the distance between two notes. The smallest interval is called a **half step**. This is the distance from any note to the next note on the keyboard regardless of whether it's a black or white key. For example, from C to C♯ or D♭ is a half step. So is from D to D♯ or E♭. So are from E to F, and from B to C. If you start with a black key a half step away is always the next white key.

The next smallest interval is called a **whole step.** A whole step equals two half steps. For example, from C to D, D to E, F to G, G to A, and A to B are all whole steps. So are such intervals as C♯ to D♯, E♭ to F, E to F♯, A♭ to B♭, and B♭ to C.

What notes can be used as grace notes?
From below, grace notes are usually a half-step below the melody note. For example if the melody note is E, the lower grace note would usually be a D♯, although D natural can sometimes be used especially when it's in the same scale as the one you're playing in.

From above, grace notes are usually a whole step or a half step above the melody note depending on the scale you're playing in. For example, in the scale of C you'd probably use the note A as an upper grace note to G. In the scale of F minor (which has four flats) you'd probably use an A♭. But these are only guidelines, not hard and fast rules.

How do I play grace notes?
It's important to remember that the grace note is played just *before* the regular melody note. That is, the melody note is played in its usual place; the time that the grace note occupies is taken from the preceding note. Ordinarily grace notes are played with a different finger than the melody note, but sometimes—especially in blues and jazz—you can slide off the grace note (if it's a black key) and strike the melody note with the same finger.

Grace notes (Cont.)

Examples of grace notes from a half step below the melody note. These always sound good.

Grace notes from a whole step below. The ones in the C scale tend to sound better to most people than those that aren't in the C scale such as B♭ and E♭.

Grace notes from a half step above. Here again, the ones in the C scale (F and C) sound better than those that aren't (A♭, B♭, D♭, E♭, and G♭).

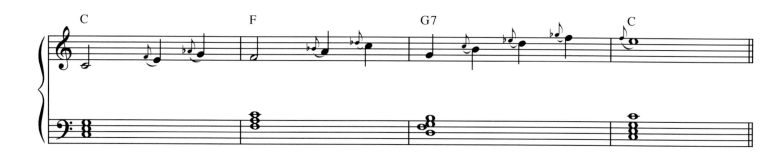

Grace notes from a whole step above. Same comments as above.

Remember that this is a book about improvisation. Just because some people may not like the sound of, say, a G♭ as a grace note to an F doesn't mean that you shouldn't use it. If it sounds right to you go with it!

Multiple Grace Notes

Two or more grace notes can also be used. These may approach the melody note from below, above, or a combination of both. When there are more than one grace note they are usually notated as small 16th notes or even 32nd notes.

Double grace ntoes from below and above.

Double grace notes from above and below.

Triple grace notes.

Quadruple grace notes.

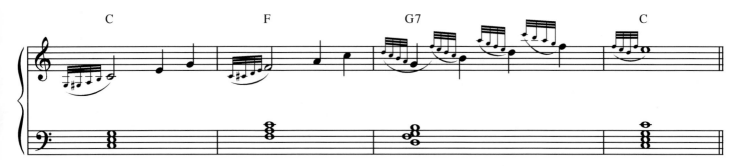

The next four sets of grace notes begin on the melody note. Then comes a higher note and finally the melody note. The first of these is called **mordent** in classical music. Its symbol is ❧.

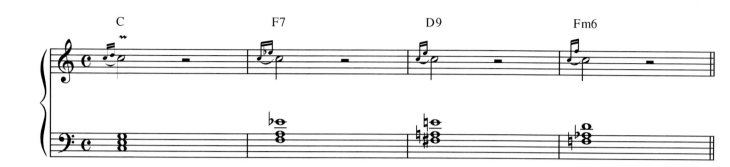

The next four embellishments insert a lower tone between two melody notes.

The first one is sometimes called an **inverted mordent** (❧).

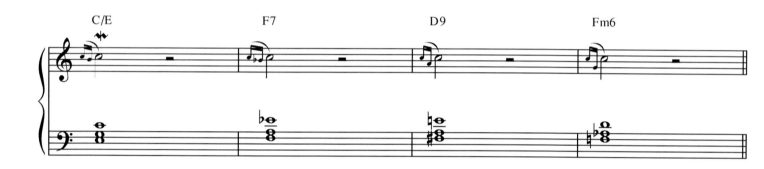

The symbol ∾ is called a **turn**. It means to play a series of four or five grace notes leading to the next note.

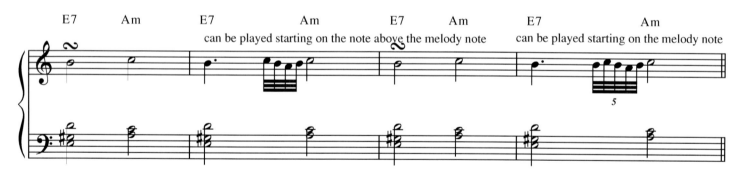

Trills are a rapid alternation between the melody note and the note above. Up till about the time of J.S. Bach they usually began on the note above. Since then they usually begin on the melody note.

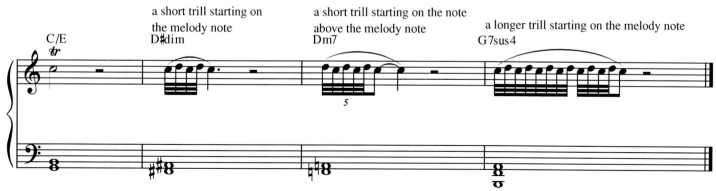

What are neighbor notes?
Neighbor notes are notes that lie a half step or a whole step above or below a melody note.

How are they notated?
They're written like any other note and are the same size as a normal note.

How are neighbor notes used?
Neighbor notes are used to enhance melody notes. When the melody note is a chord tone it tends to sound a little bland, like scrambled eggs without salt. Adding a neighbor note gives the melody more interest and spice.

Are they played fast, like grace notes?
No. Although they can be played almost as fast as a grace note, a better effect is to play them at least as long as an 8th note. They can be as long as the melody note or even longer. See examples below.

Using the same simple melody you learned on page 6, here are ways you can use upper neighbor notes (UN) and lower neighbor notes (LN) to enhance it.

 Track 2

Example 10B.1. Upper neighbors. All the other notes are chord tones.

Example 10B.2. Lower neighbors, some of which are not in the scale.

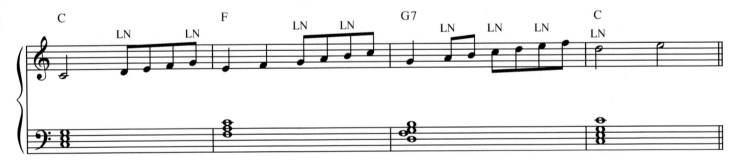

Example 10B.3. Lower neighbors that are a half step below the melody note.

Here are four more variations mixing upper and lower neighbors. After completing this page, make up some original variations using the same techniques. You can use either the same four-bar melody, or pick a favorite tune and see what you can do with it.

This variation may sound a little strange to you. It uses many chromatic (not in the scale) neighbor notes.

This variation uses a steady stream of 8th notes, all of which are in the scale. It's typical of certain styles including Celtic and Bluegrass (which see later in this book).

What is a passing tone?
A passing tone (PT) is a non-chord tone that connects two chord tones by step.

Example 12B.1. The passing tones (PT) connect the chord tones by step

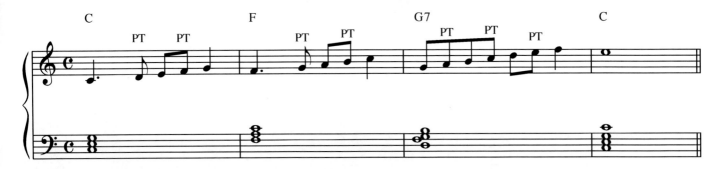

How does a passing tone differ from a neighbor note?
You can skip to a neighbor note from any chord tone. Passing tones are always approached by step.

Example 12B.2. Passing tones are approached by step. Neighbor notes can be approached by skip. (A skip is more than a whole step...three or more half steps.)

What is a diatonic passing tone?
The word diatonic simply means "in the scale." All the examples on this page are diatonic passing tones. Remember that the chord tones in a C chord are C E G; in an F chord, F A C; in a G7 chord, G B D F.

Example 12B.3. Diatonic passing tones and neighbor notes on the same melody.

Example 12B.4. More neighbor notes and passing tones

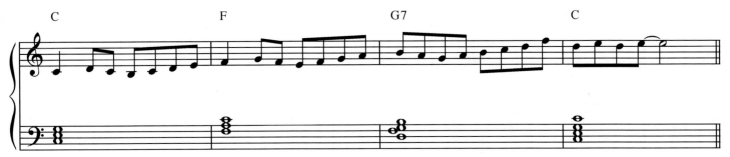

What is a chromatic passing tone?

Chromatic passing tones connect chord tones by half steps. For example, if two chord tones are C and E, the chromatic passing tones between them would be C#, D, and D#. To put it another way, all the black and white keys in between the chord tones are used.

Here's a new melody based on the same chords. We've broken up the chords into individual notes to add a little interest to the left hand.

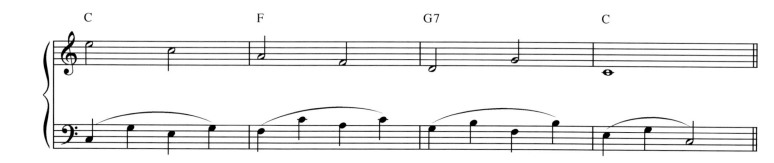

This variation uses diatonic passing tones.

This variation uses chromatic passing tones to connect the melody notes.

Improvising with Melodies—Summing Up

So far in this book we have used the melody as the basis of all our variations. We have learned three different techniques for enhancing and varying a given melody:

Grace notes:
> Grace notes from a half step and a whole step below the melody note.
> Grace notes from a half step and a whole step above the melody note.
> Double grace notes from below and above.
> Triple and quadruple grace notes from above and below.
> Mordents, inverted mordents, turns and trills.

Neighbor notes:
> Diatonic neighbor notes from below and above the melody note.
> Chromatic neighbor notes from below and above the melody note.

Passing tones:
> Diatonic passing tones
> Chromatic passing tones

We suggest that you take a favorite tune and experiment with these techniques till you find variations that please you. Not every technique works on every tune. For example, most people would not consider a classical melody a suitable place to use improvisation. But who knows, you might be the person who figures out a new sound that combines classical melodies with techniques associated with rock and jazz (as did the group *Mannheim Steamroller* and the vocal group *Amici Forever*).

A word of caution:
These—and any—techniques can add interest and spice to your playing, but must not be overused. Embellishments, especially grace notes and trills become annoying mannerisms when heard too often. Like salt in your scrambled eggs, just because a little is good doesn't mean that a lot is better!

A Bit of Music Theory

What is a scale?
A scale is a series of tones that begins on the note that names the scale (called the root, tonic, or keynote) and ends on the same note an octave (eight notes) higher. For example, a C scale begins on the note C and continues up through D, E, F, G, A, B, and finally another C.

What is an interval?
An interval is the space between two notes. To determine the name of an interval, just count on your fingers. The lower note is "1." Then count up the scale till you get to the note you want. For example, the interval between C and D is called a second. Between C and E the interval is a third. Between C and G is a fifth, and between C and the next higher C is eight notes called an octave.

What is the interval of a half step?
We've already discussed this interval on page 6, but to review: a half step is the distance between any note on the keyboard and the very next note regardless of whether it's a white or a black key.

What is the interval of a whole step?
A whole step, also called a major second, is two half steps. From the white keys C, D, F, G, or A, a whole step is the next white key. From the black keys Db, Gb, or Ab a whole step is the next black key.

Why do I need to know this?
Because scales are composed of a series of whole steps and half steps. So to understand scales, you should understand intervals.

How many kinds of scales are there?
There are hundreds of scales, but don't panic! Only a few different ones are used in most of the music you might hear. Most folk songs and bluegrass, all of country and western music and most jazz are written in either the major or minor scale. Examples of the most useful major and minor scales can be found on the following pages. Later in the book we'll also teach you some exotic scales used in Gypsy, Klezmer, Japanese, and Chinese musics.

What is a chord?
A chord is a group of three or more tones that sound good together. It may be useful to think of the most common chords as being built in intervals of a third. For example, the C major chord can be thought of as the 1st, 3rd, and 5th notes of the C major scale, namely C E G. (Notice that from C to E is the interval of a third, and from E to G is also a third.) The F major chord can be thought of as the 4th, 6th, and 8th notes of the C major scale, namely F A C. Notice that these also are separated by thirds. The chord G7 (say "G seventh") can be thought of as the 5th, 7th, 2nd, and 4th notes of the C major scale, G B D F.

What are the I, IV, and V7 chords?
In the key of C, because it begins on the first note of the scale, the C major chord is sometimes called the I chord (say "the one chord.") Similarly, because the F chord is built on the 4th step of the scale it's sometimes called the IV chord (the four chord.) Since G7 is built on the 5th step of the scale it's sometimes called the V7 (five-seven) chord.

Why are these chords important?
The I, IV, and V7 chords are the most important chords in any major or minor key. Hundreds—and probably thousands—of songs can be accompanied using these three chords.

What is a major scale?

A major scale consists of eight notes: The root or keynote which is followed by an ascending series of whole steps and half steps until the higher keynote is reached. For example, the C major scale consists of the notes C D E F G A B C.

In what order are the whole steps and half steps?

In a major scale (and only in a major scale!) the intervals occur in this order: whole step, whole step, half step, whole step, whole step, whole step, half step. If you've done it right you should now be at the keynote again.

Can you give me a "for instance?"

From C to D is a whole step; from D to E is a whole step; from E to F is a half step; from F to G, G to A, and A to B are all whole steps; from B up to C is a half step. An easy way to remember this is "2 and a half, 3 and a half."

Here's a useful table showing all possible half steps, whole steps, minor 3rds (three half steps) and major 3rds (four half steps) and perfect 5ths (7 half steps).

Root	Half Step	Whole Step	Minor 3rd	Major 3rd	Fifth
C	C♯ or D♭	D	E♭	E	G
C♯	D	D♯	E	E♯	G♯
D♭	D	E♭	F♭	F	A♭
D	D♯ or E♭	E	F	F♯	A
E♭	E	F	G♭	G	B♭
E	F	F♯	G	G♯	B
F	F♯ or G♭	G	A♭	A	C
F♯	G	G♯	A	A♯	C♯
G♭	G	A♭	B♭♭ or A	B♭	D♭
G	G♯ or A♭	A	B♭	B	D
A♭	A	B♭	C♭	C	E♭
A	A♯ or B♭	B	C	C♯	E
B♭	B or C♭	C	D♭	D	F
B	C	C♯	D	D♯	F♯
C♭	C	D♭	E♭♭ or D	E♭	G♭

Major Scales

The following are all the possible major scales. The whole steps and half steps are clearly marked. The numbers below indicate the scale steps. These scales are for reference only and need not be played.

C major scale: no sharps or flats.

C♯ major scale: all notes are sharp.

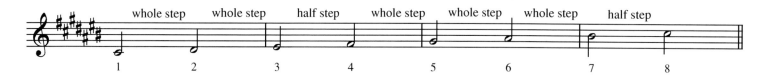

D♭ major scale: B, E, A, D, and G are flat.

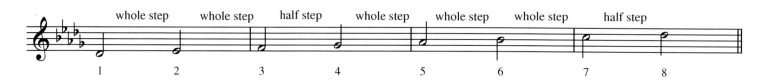

The D major scale: F and C are sharp.

E♭ major scale: B, E, and A are flat.

E major scale: F, C, G, and D are sharp.

F major scale: B is flat.

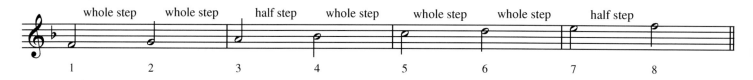

F# major scale: F, C, G, D, A, and E are sharp.

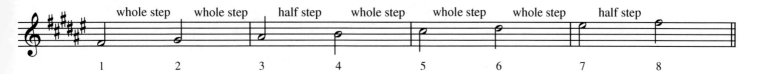

Gb major scale: B, E, A, D, G, and C are flat.

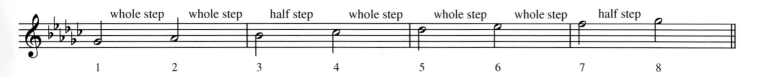

G major scale: F is sharp.

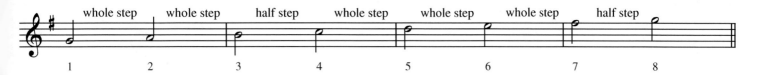

Ab major scale: B, E, A, and D are flat.

A major scale: F, C, and G are sharp.

Bb major scale: B and E are flat.

B major scale: F, C, G, D, and A are sharp.

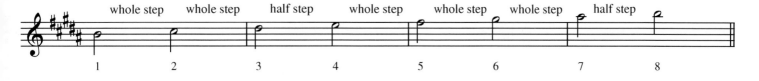

Cb major scale: all notes are flat.

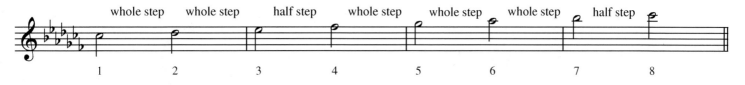

How can I use major scales to improvise?

You can use major scales to improvise with in two ways:

1. If you're still using the melody as your basis, you can use scales to fill the spaces between the melody notes. Just make sure the scale you're using is the same one the piece is written in. Ex. 20.1 is a basic melody in the key of G. It has large skips in it, so Ex. 20.2 demonstrates how you can use the G major scale (G A B C D E F♯ G) to fill in the gaps between the melody notes. The accompanying chords in the key of G are the I, IV, and V7 chords: G (G B D), C (C E G), and D7 (D F♯ A C).

Example 20.1. Basic melody in the key of G.

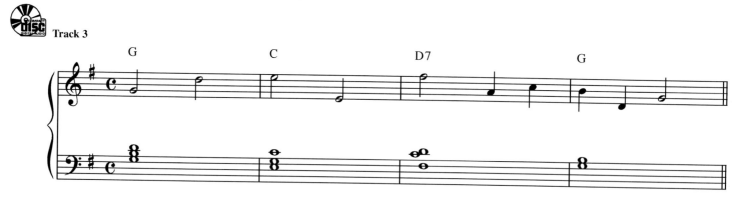

Example 20.2. Using the G major scale to fill the spaces between melody notes.

Another way to improvise is to ignore the melody and run the scale. This technique is often used after the melody has been established. For example, on the first chorus play the melody with a few variations. Second chorus, play the melody again, but with added passing tones and neighbor notes. Third (and other choruses), play variations based on the scale, but not suggesting the melody. Last chorus, play the melody again with or without an added final section called by its Italian name, "Coda".

Example 20.3 uses as its basis the same G major melody, but ignores the actual melody notes and uses the G major scale to develop variations.

Ignoring the melody notes and running the G major scale.

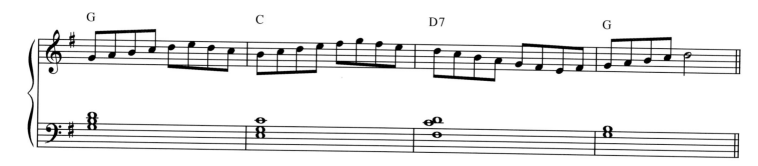

Here is an improvisation on a familiar tune in the key of G. This variation uses the G major scale as well as other techniques you have learned such as grace notes, neighbor notes, etc. The accompanying chords are the I, IV, and V7 chords in the G: G, C, D7 plus one other chord, A7, which is spelled A C# E G.

Jingle Bells (free variation)

Now it's your turn. Use the rhythm track on the CD to play your own variations.

What are minor scales?

When you hear the word "minor" in music you should always think "lowered third." For example, the third note of the G *major* scale is B; the third note of the G *minor* scale is B♭. The third note of the D *major* scale is F♯; the third note of the D *minor* scale is F natural. That is, the third is lowered by a half step.

Does this apply to chords also?

Yes. The third of a C *major* chord is E; the third of a C *minor* chord is E♭. The third of an A7 chord is C♯; the third of an A *minor* 7th chord is C natural.

How many kinds of minor scale are there?

There are three kinds of minor scale in common use: the **natural minor**, the **harmonic minor**, and the **melodic minor**.

How do you determine the key signature of a minor scale?

Minor scales borrow their key signature from the major scale which is three half steps higher. For example, the G minor scale has the same key signature (two flats) as the B♭ major scale. The E minor scale has the same key signature as G major, one sharp. Because they share the same key signature, E minor is called the relative minor of G major, conversely, G major is the relative major of E minor.

What is a natural minor scale?

Since the B♭ major scale uses a key signature of two flats, B♭ and E♭, the G minor scale uses the same key signatures but starts and ends on G. the notes in a G natural minor scale are G A B♭ C D E♭ F G. We'll discuss the natural minor in greater detail in the section on modes.

What is a harmonic minor scale?

The harmonic minor is the same as the natural minor except that the 7th note of the scale is raised a half step. In the G natural minor scale the 7th note is F, so the G harmonic minor scale uses an F♯ instead of an F. The notes in a G harmonic minor scale are G A B♭ D E♭ F♯ G. The B♭ and E♭ are usually in the key signature, but the F♯ is written in every time it appears.

Why is it called "harmonic"?

Because the chords are derived from the scale. The most important chords in each harmonic minor scale are the I, IV, and V7 chords, just like in the major scale. But in a minor scale both the I and IV chords are minor instead of major; the V7 is an ordinary seventh chord, the same as in major. For example, the I chord in the key of G minor is a G minor chord (G B♭ D); The IV chord is a C minor chord (C E♭ G). The V7 chord is a D7 chord (D F♯ A C).

On the next two pages you'll find the most useful harmonic minor scales with the half steps, whole steps, and in one case one-and-a-half steps marked. These are for reference only and need not be practiced.

22

Harmonic Minor Scales

The A harmonic minor scale. Has the same key signature as C major, no sharps or flats...

The Bb harmonic minor scale has the same key signature as Db major, so B, E, A, D, and G are flat...

The B harmonic minor scale has the same signature as D major: F and C are sharp.

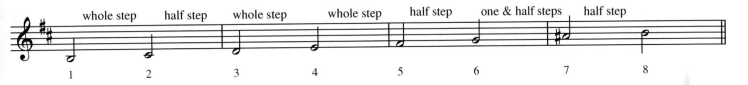

The C harmonic minor scale has the same key signature as Eb major: B, E, and A are flat.

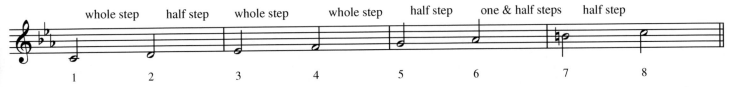

The C# harmonic minor scale has the same key signature as E major: F, C, G, and D are sharp.

The D harmonic minor scale has the same key signature as F major: B is flat.

The D# harmonic minor scale has the same key signature as F# major: F, C, G, D, A, and E are sharp.

Harmonic Minor Scales (Cont.)

The E♭ harmonic minor scale has the same key signature as G♭ major: B, E, A, D, G, and C are flat.

The E harmonic minor scale has the same key signature as G major: F is sharp.

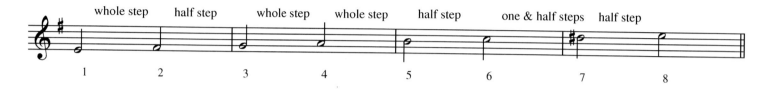

The F harmonic minor scale has the same key signature as A♭ major: B, E, A, and D are flat.

The F♯ harmonic minor scale has the same key signature as A major: F, C, and G are sharp.

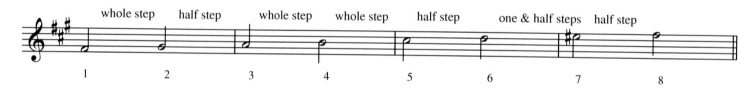

The G harmonic minor scale has the same key signature as B♭ major: B and E are flat.

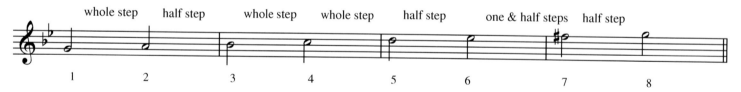

The G♯ harmonic minor scale has the same key signature as B major: F, C, G, D, and A are sharp.

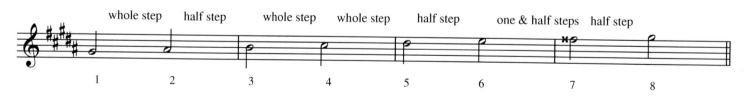

The A♭ harmonic minor scale has the same key signature as C♭ major: All seven notes are flat.

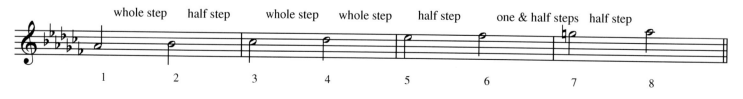

Improvising with Harmonic Minor Scales

Any of the techniques you've learned so far can be used in minor as well as major. Here is a short example: first the basic melody in D minor, then a series of four-bar variations that use many of the techniques you've learned so far. The left hand uses the I IV and V7 chords: D minor (D F A), G minor (G B♭ D), and A7 (A C♯ E G).

Basic Melody

Track 4

1st variation sticks fairly close to the melody

2nd variation uses upper and lower neighbor notes to the basic melody. Accompanying chords are broken into half notes to add more motion to the left hand. More about this later in the book.

3rd variation ignores melody and just runs the scale. Accompanying chords are broken into quarter notes to add still more motion.

Melodic Minor Scales

As the name implies, melodic minor scales are often used to construct melodies. Like other minors, the melodic minor borrows its key signature from the major scale one and a half steps higher. Unlike other minors, the melodic minor has two forms: Ascending, the 6th and 7th steps are each raised a half step. In the descending form, the 6th and 7th steps revert to their natural state.

The A melodic minor scale: same key signature as C major, no sharps or flats.

The Bb melodic minor scale: same signature as Db major, B, E, A, D, and G are flat.

The B melodic minor scale: same signature as D major, F and c are sharp.

The C melodic minor scale: same signature as Eb major, B, E, and A are flat.

The C♯ melodic minor scale: same signature as E major, F, C, G, and D are sharp.

The D melodic minor scale: same signature as F major, B is flat.

The D♯ melodic minor scale: same signature as F♯ major, F, C, G, D, A and E are sharp.

The Eb melodic minor scale: same signature as Gb major, B, E, A, D, G, and C are flat.

The E melodic minor scale: same signature as G major, F is sharp.

The F melodic minor scale: same signature as Ab major, B, E, A, and D are flat.

The F# melodic minor scale: same signature as A major, F, C, and G are sharp.

The G melodic minor scale: same signature as Bb major, B and E are flat.

The G# melodic minor scale: same signature as B major, F, C, G, D, and A are sharp.

The Ab melodic minor scale: same signature as Cb major, all notes are flat.

Improvising with the Melodic Minor Scale

Below is a melody in A minor, followed by four-bar variations that make use of many of the techniques you have learned. When using the melodic minor, the three basic chords are still I, IV, and V7, but the IV chord is sometimes major. I = A minor (A C E), IV = D minor (D F A) or D major (D F♯ A), V7 = E7 (E G♯ B D).

1st variation sticks fairly close to the melody

2nd variation uses diatonic and chromatic neighbor notes and passing tones

3rd variation ignores the melody notes and runs the scale.

Now it's your turn. Create your own variations with the rhythm track on the CD.

28

Improvising with Modes

What are modes?
Modes are a series of notes separated by whole steps and half steps. Like scales, they begin and end on notes an octave apart.

How do modes differ from scales?
Sometimes modes are the same as certain scales. Other modes have the half steps and whole steps in varying places.

When were modes invented?
Their origins are lost in history, but they probably were in use 2500 or more years ago.

When did they fall out of use?
Modes were the common form of musical expression until about the 16th century when they were gradually replaced by major and minor scales. Virtually all classical music, popular, and folk songs composed between 1650 and 1900 were written in major or minor scales.

Why study them now?
About a hundred years ago modes were rediscovered, and because they had a different sound from major and minor scales, they sounded fresh and unusual. Many rock tunes are written in modes (e.g. The Beatles' "Paperback Writer") and it is possible to find old folk songs that apparently date from the days when modes were in common use (e.g. "Scarborough Fair").

How many modes are there?
There are seven modes, six of which are still in use. Modes are named after places in ancient Greece.

What are the seven modes and what notes does each one contain?
Originally the modes used only the natural notes (notes without sharps or flats). Or, you can think of them as consisting of the white keys on the piano.

The **Ionian (Eye-o-nee-an) mode** is identical to the C major scale: C D E F G A B C

The **Dorian (Dor-ee-an) mode** uses the notes D E F G A B C D

The **Phrygian (Fridj-ee-an) mode** uses the notes E F G A B D E

The **Lydian (Lid-ee-an) mode** uses the notes F G A B C D E F

The **Mixolydian (Mix-o-lid-ee-an) mode** uses the notes G A B C D E F G

The **Aeolian (Ay-oh-lee-an) mode** is the same as the A natural minor scale: A B C D E F G A

The **Locrian (Low-cree-an) mode** (rarely if ever used) uses the notes B C D E F G A B

On the next few pages we describe each mode in detail and give examples of improvisations based on them.

The Ionian Mode

The Ionian mode is the same as the C major scale: C D E F G A B C. The most important chords in this mode are the I chord C (C E G), the IV chord F (F A C), and the V7 chord G7 (G B D F). Here is an improvisation in the Ionian mode. After you learn it, try your own improvisation against the rhythm track.

Track 5

Ionian Item

The Dorian Mode

On the keyboard, the Dorian mode consists of the white keys between D and D an octave higher: D E F G A B C D. This sea chantey is in the Dorian mode. The I chord in the Dorian mode is D minor (D F A). Other important chords are the VII chord (C E G) the III chord F (F A C) and the IV chord G (G B D).

The Drunken Sailor

After you learn this tune and variation, try to develop your own improvisation using the Dorian mode.

The Phrygian Mode

This mode is closely associated with Spanish music, especially flamenco. It consists of the notes E F G A B C D E. The most important chords in the Phrygian mode are the IV chord A minor (A C E), the III chord G (G B D), the II chord F (F A C) and the I chord which is almost always played as E major (E G♯ B) although technically the note G♯ is not in the mode. Here is a typical four-bar sequence and three variations on it.

The Spanish Tinge

Basic Melody

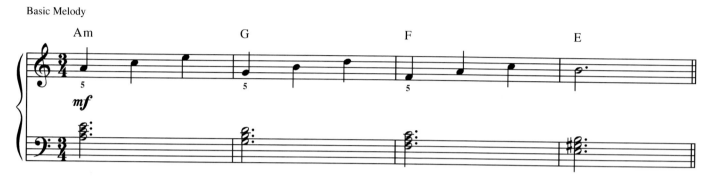

1st variation sticks close to the melody

2nd variation is more free using passing tones and neighbor notes

3rd variation ignores melody and just runs the mode freely

After you learn this melody and variations, try your hand at making up your own.

The Lydian mode

The Lydian mode is like an F major scale but with a B natural instead of a B♭. The B natural gives it a pungent sound that some jazz players like. It is also characteristic of some Hungarian folk music and shows up in the music of Bela Bartok, Zoltan Kodaly and others... The notes in the Lydian mode are F G A B C D E F. The main chords are the I chord F (F A C), the II chord G (G B D) and the V chord C (C E G).

 Track 6

Lydia's Lunch

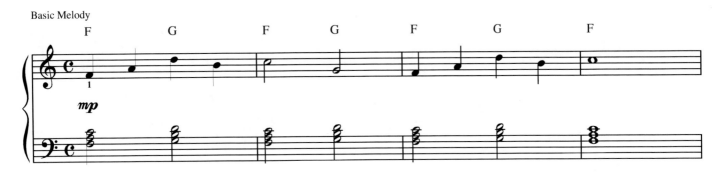

The Mixolydian Mode

This mode is like a G major scale that uses F natural instead of F♯. The notes are G A B C D E F G. To illustrate this mode we have chosen "Old Joe Clark," a famous square dance tune which is in the Mixolydian mode. The most important chords are the I chord G (G B D) and the VII chord F (F A C).

Old Joe Clark

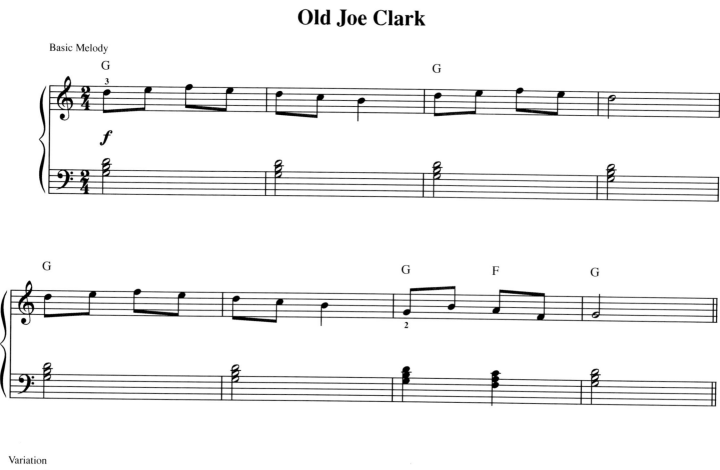

The Aeolian mode

This ancient mode tends to have a sweet, sad sound, as in the famous Civil War song "When Johnny Comes Marching Home" (which probably was based on a Celtic melody). We've chosen an old folk song to illustrate the Aeolian mode. The notes are A B C D E F G A. The main chords are the I chord A minor (A C E), the VII chord G (G B D), the III chord C (C E G,) the VI chord F (F A C), and the V chord E minor or major (E G B or E G# B).

Shady Grove

The Locrian Mode
This mode consists of the notes B C D E F G A B. Because the dissonant interval B-F is so prominent, ancient musicians found the mode unusable unless the F was sharped or the B was flatted. If the F is sharped, the mode sounds exactly like a Phrygian mode starting on B. If the B is flatted, it sounds like a Lydian mode starting on B♭. However, it is interesting to note that the accidentals F♯ and B♭ are still the most commonly used. F♯ is the first sharp in a key signature that uses sharps. B♭ is the first flat in a key signature that uses flats. But since this mode is so rare or duplicates other modes, there's no need to concern ourselves with it here.

Can modes be transposed to other notes?
In ancient usage the modes were always played on the notes we have described. But nowadays a mode can start on any note as long as the half steps and whole steps remain in the same relative places.

Can you give me an example?
The Dorian mode consists of the notes D E F G A B C D. All the steps in this mode are whole steps except for E-F and B-C which are half steps. Since these occur between the 2nd to 3rd steps and between the 6th to 7th steps, when you start the mode on a different note, sharps or flats must be added so that the half steps still fall between the 2nd and 3rd steps and between the 6th and 7th steps. We don't have room to illustrate every possibility, but the examples below will suggest how to go about transposing modes to other notes.

The six most important modes, what notes they contain, where the half steps lie, and which are the most important chords (key chord in bold face type).
The Ionian mode: C D E F G A B C half steps between the 3rd and 4th steps and the 7th and 8th steps; most important chords **C** F G

The Dorian mode: D E F G A B C D half steps between the 2nd and 3rd steps and the 6th and 7th steps; most important chords **Dm** G C F

The Phrygian mode: E F G A B C D E half steps between the 1st and 2nd steps and the 5th and 6th steps; most important chords Am G F **E major or minor**

The Lydian mode: F G A B C D E F half steps between the 4th and 5th and the 7th and 8th steps; most important chords **F** G C

The Mixolydian mode: G A B C D E F half steps between the 3rd and 4th and the 6th and 7th steps; most important chords **G** F C

The Aeolian mode: A B C D E F G A half steps between the 2nd and 3rd and the 5th and 6th steps; most important chords **Am** G Dm C

Some Examples of Various Modes Starting on Other Notes

Improvising with Specialty Scales

So far, all the scales and modes we've studied have one thing in common: they contain seven different notes. But many tunes—especially folk songs—use other scales with fewer notes. For example, the American murder ballad *Pretty Polly* is based on a six-note scale sometimes called a hexachord or "gapped" scale. In this case the hexachord consists of the notes D E F G A C. That is, it's just like the Dorian mode, but with the 6th step (B) omitted. You may find that your improvisations will sound more authentic if you limit them to the notes in this hexachord.

Track 7

Pretty Polly

I used to be a rambler and I strayed from town to town,
I used to be a rambler and I strayed from town to town,
I courted Pretty Polly and her beauty's never been found.

I courted Pretty Polly the livelong night,
I courted Pretty Polly the livelong night,
Then left her the next morning before it was light.

What is a pentatonic scale?

As its name implies, the pentatonic scale contains only five notes. For example, the C pentatonic scale consists of the notes C D E G and A. That is, it's just like the C major scale with the 4th and 7th steps omitted.

Why is this scale very important?

Pentatonic scales are used in the music of many peoples around the world especially in Chinese, American Indian, South American, and African music. But even more importantly, it is a resource for improvising. This is because when you use, say, an F pentatonic scale against an F chord, *any* note you play will sound good. It's impossible to make a mistake! For example, the first section of *Oh Susanna* is based on the F pentatonic scale; it uses only the notes F G A C and D. The variation that follows also uses the same notes, but in different combinations.

Oh Susanna

And did you notice that if you confine your playing to the black keys, you're actually playing a G♭ pentatonic scale? That's why the key of G♭—although having the difficult key signature of six flats—is a good key in which to improvise on the piano.

The next folk song is based on the C pentatonic scale: C D E G A.

Shortnin' Bread

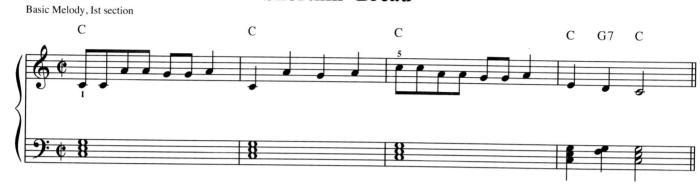

1st variation uses only notes in the C pentatonic scale

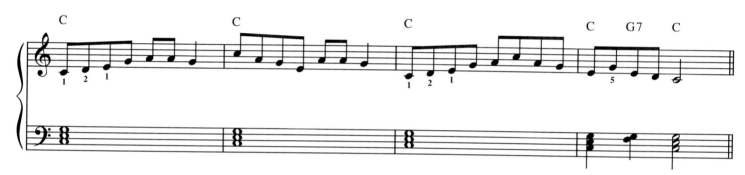

2nd variation uses notes of the C pentatonic scale but expands into the upper register. Follow the fingering carefully for best results.

3rd variation adds chromatic (not in the scale) neighbor notes. Notice how the introduction of notes that are not in the scale completely changes the effect of the improvisation.

Did you like the sound of the D♯ and F♯. This is one way to show your individuality as a musician. Use chromatic neighbor notes if you like the sound. If not, don't. But if you don't like the sound give yourself a chance to get used to it. Sometimes it takes a while.

Incredible as it might seem, some songs use only four notes, yet can have a terrific emotional impact. This Appalachian ballad uses only the notes A C D and E (called a tetrachord), yet the legendary folksinger, Leadbelly, and Kurt Cobain of Nirvana both recorded very powerful versions. Here is the chorus and a variation.

In the Pines

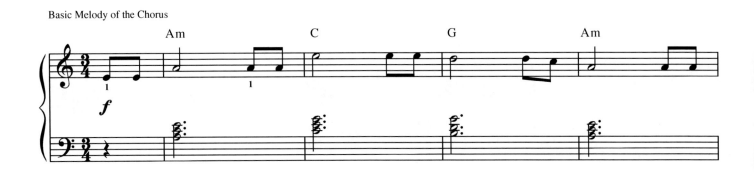

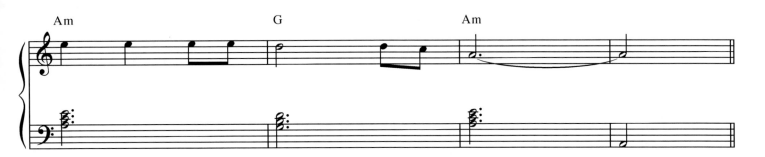

Although it is possible to improvise using only four notes, it is rather limiting. In this variation we have added B and G to the tetrachord A C D E to form an A minor hexachord, A B C D E G A.

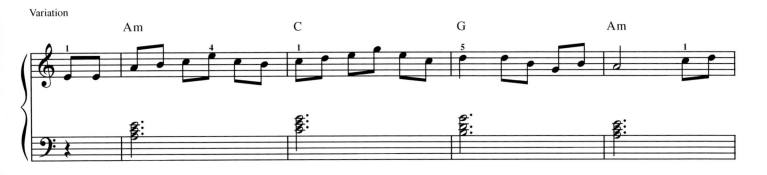

41

Improvising by Adding Notes to a Melody

How many notes can be added to a melody note?
As many you can finger comfortably.

Why add notes to a melody?
Adding notes make a melody sound richer and fuller. They are used in every type of music from classical to Bluegrass.

How do I know which added notes will sound good?
To answer this question we'll need to go into a little music theory. When adding a single note to a melody, the general rules are these:

If the melody note is a chord tone, the added note should be a chord tone.

Example 41.1. In this example the melody note is always a chord tone. The added note below the melody is also a chord tone. Remember the spelling of the basic chords in the key of C: C=C E G; F=F A C; G7=G B D F.

If the melody note is a diatonic (in the scale) neighbor note or passing tone, the added note should be a diatonic neighbor note or passing tone.

Example 41.2. The same melody with added diatonic neighbor notes (N) and passing tones (PT).

If the melody note is a chromatic (not in the scale) neighbor note or passing tone, the added note should be a chromatic neighbor note or passing tone. (Example 41.3)

Example 41.3. The same melody with added chromatic neighbor notes (N) and passing tones (PT).

(These examples are for illustration only and need not be practiced.)

Should the added note be above or below the melody?
The ear tends to pick out the higher note as the melody, so adding a note below the melody is always good. A note can also be added above the melody, but you need good control to bring out the lower melody note. However, if the melody is well-known you can assume that your listeners will be able to pick it out without difficulty.

You'll find some practical examples of these techniques on the next two pages.

Here's a country style tune that's arranged entirely with single notes added below the melody. Especially notice the use of diatonic and chromatic passing tones in both the melody and harmony. For a better effect play the eighth notes long-short, long-short instead of evenly.

Just Lopin' Along

This waltz, which is the Missouri state song, is arranged using double notes with the melody sometimes above and sometimes below. Pay special attention to the use of chromatic neighbor notes in both the melody and harmony. For better effect, play the eighth notes long-short long-short instead of even.

The Missouri Waltz

John Eppel

Using a Note Above the Melody as a Drone

A very nice effect can be obtained by using a repeated note above the melody as a drone or pedal point. The higher note is played with each melody note regardless of whether the drone fits with the chord. In this arrangement the drone is the note A; the melody is always below it. The accompanying chords are the I, IV, and V7 in the key of D: D=D F♯ A; G=G B D; A7=A C♯ E G.

Black-Eyed Susie

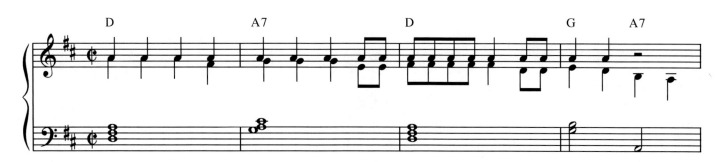

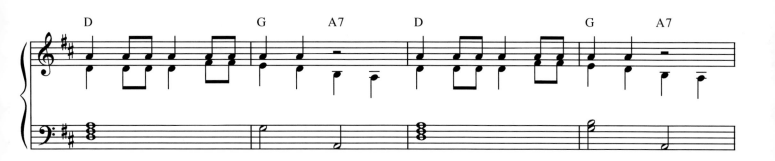

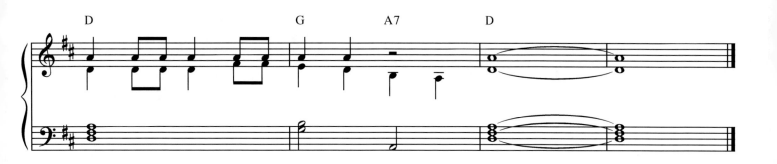

All I want in this creation's
A pretty little wife and a big plantation
Chorus:
Hey, little black-eyed Susie,
Hey, little black-eyed Susie,
Hey, little black-eyed Susie, hey!

Love my wife, I love my baby
Love my biscuits sopped in gravy
Chorus:
Hey, little black-eyed Susie,
Hey, little black-eyed Susie,
Hey, little black-eyed Susie, hey!

Improvising with Chords

What is a chord?
A chord is a group of three or more different notes that sound good together. For example, the C major chord consists of the notes C, E, and G. The D minor chord contains the notes D, F, and A. The G7 chord contains the notes G, B, D, and F. These notes can occur in any order; the C chord can be spelled C E G, E G C, G C E, E C G and so on. Notes can also be doubled: The C chord can have two C's, two E's, and/or two G's.

What kinds of chords are there?

There are dozens of different types of chords, but the overwhelming majority of the ones you'll need are either major, minor, or 7th chords.

How are chords spelled?
Chords are generally built in intervals of a third. For example, the C chord (when not specified, we're always talking about a major chord) consists of the notes C E G. From C to E is a major third (two whole steps or four half steps); from E to G is a minor third (a whole step and a half step or three half steps). On the other hand, the D minor chord which has the notes D F A has a minor third between D and F, and a major third between F and A. The G7 chord takes a G major chord (G B D) and adds another minor third above it (F).

Here is a chart that tells you how to spell every possible major, minor, and seventh chord. The more important ones are in bold face type.

Root tone	Major Chord	Minor Chord	Seventh Chord
C	**C E G**	**C E♭ G**	**C E G B♭**
C♯	C♯ E♯ G♯	C♯ E G♯	C♯ E♯ G♯ B
D♭	D♭ F A♭	D♭ F♭ A♭	D♭ F A♭ C♭
D	**D F♯ A**	**D F A**	**D F♯ A C**
E♭	E♭ G B♭	E♭ G♭ B♭	E♭ G B♭ D♭
E	**E G♯ B**	**E G B**	**E G♯ B D**
F	**F A C**	**F A♭ C**	**F A C E♭**
F♯	F♯ A♯ C♯	F♯ A C♯	F♯ A♯ C♯ E
G♭	G♭ B♭ D♭	G♭ B♭♭ (A) D♭	G♭ B♭ D♭ F♭
G	**G B D**	**G B♭ D**	**G B D F**
A♭	A♭ C E♭	A♭ C♭ E♭	A♭ C E♭ G♭
A	**A C♯ E**	**A C E**	**A C♯ E G**
B♭	B♭ D F	B♭ D♭ F	B♭ D F A♭
B	**B D♯ F♯**	**B D F♯**	**B D♯ F♯ A**
C♭	C♭ E♭ G♭	C♭ E♭♭ (D) G♭	C♭ E♭ G♭ B♭♭ (A)

Using Chords as Tools for Improvisation

Chords are very important building blocks of most kinds of music, and a knowledge of them is indispensable for creating convincing improvisations. As we've previously stated, most ordinary chords have either three or four different notes. These notes are named for the position they occupy in their respective scale. For example, the C major chord contains the notes C, E, and G. In the C scale (C D E F G A G C), C is the first step (called the root or tonic), E is the third step, and G is the fifth step. So we can infer that **major chords** consist of the root, third, and fifth notes of a major scale. (You can refer back to the major scales on pages 17 and 18.)

Minor chords are identical to major chords except that the third has been lowered a half step. For example, C major = C E G; C minor = C E♭ G. Another example: D major = D F♯ A; D minor = D F A.

Seventh chords can be thought of as the root, third, fifth, and **lowered seventh** of a major scale. For example, the G7 chord contains the notes G B D F. In the G major scale (G A B C D E F♯ G) the root is G, the third is B, the fifth is D, and the flatted seventh is F natural. The C7 chord consists of the root, third, fifth, and flatted seventh of the C major scale: C E G B♭.

Inversions
You already know that the notes of a chord can be put in any order. This means that any chord can be played with any of its notes in the bass (that is, as the lowest note). For example, the G7 chord can be played with a G, a B, a D, or an F as the lowest note. These are called different inversions. A chord that has the root as the lowest note is said to be in root position. If the third is the lowest note the chord is in 1st inversion. If the fifth is the lowest note the chord is in 2nd inversion. If the seventh is the lowest note the chord is in 3rd inversion.

How to use chords in the right hand
You've already learned how to enhance a melody by adding a single harmony note. Now you can create a full chord (three or four notes) by adding notes below the melody note. If the melody note is a chord tone, the added notes should also be chord tones. If the melody is a passing tone or neighbor chord, you have several options:

  1) leave that note as a single note.

  2) create a passing chord or neighbor chord.

  3) add the neighbor note or passing tone to the existing chord.

Take a look at the facing page for examples of how to do this. (When adding chords to the right hand it's often a good idea to simplify the left hand to one or two notes.)

How to use chords in the left hand
So far in this book we have used very simple patterns in the left hand. On pages 48 and 49 you'll find examples of how to create more interesting left-hand accompaniment patterns. These are always based on the chords that accompany the melody. You can use single notes, two-note intervals, three or four note chords and endless variations on these basics.

Adding Chords to the Right-Hand Melody

If every melody note is a chord tone, just add two more notes below to make a three-part chord. When playing a seventh chord, it is usual to omit the fifth to make the fingering more practical. We'll illustrate this technique with the first four measures of an old cowboy tune.

Track 9

Red River Valley

In this variation we have added chord tones below the melody notes. Also notice that we've simplified the bass to single notes.

This old bar-room ballad starts out with many neighbor notes and passing tones. Here are two ways of dealing with them.

My Melancholy Baby

Of course, you can also just leave them as single notes. It's perfectly O.K. to mix single note passages with chords.

Here are a few ways of playing the left-hand accompaniment when the chords are C F G7 C and the meter is 4/4.

1. Play the chords as whole notes.

2. Play the chords as half notes.

3. Break up the chords into quarter notes. Sometimes called the Alberti bass.

4. Choose single notes (usually the root and fifth) and play them on the 1st and 3rd beats.

5. Play bass notes on the 1st and 3rd beats, and the rest of the chord on the 2nd and 4th beats.

6. Same as No.3, but with the notes of the chords widely spaced.

7. Break up the chords into 8th notes. Use only at slower tempos.

8. Break up chords into 8th notes with the notes of the chords widely spaced.

This barely scratches the surfaces of what's possible, because it only uses chord tones. Later in the book we'll show you how to use passing tones and neighbor notes to give your accompaniments some spice.

Here are some possibilities in 3/4 using the same C F G7 C progression.

1. Play the chords as dotted half notes.

2. Break up the chords into quarter notes.

3. Play a single note (usually the root or fifth of the chord) on the down beat. It can be a dotted half, half note or quarter note.

4. Play a quarter note on the first beat and complete the chord on the 2nd and 3rd beats. This is the so-called "oom-pah-pah" effect used for waltzes.

5. Play a quarter note on beat 1, complete the chord on beat 2, play a different quarter note on beat 3.

6. Break the chords into 8th notes.

7. Another way to break the chords into 8th notes.

8. Break the chords into 8th notes using wide spacing.

Now we suggest you go back to tunes you've already learned in this book and apply some of these styles to them. Or, find some favorite tunes and work out your own accompaniments.

A final page of accompaniment patterns, this time in 2/4. The chord progression is still C F G7 C.

1. Play each chord as a half note.

2. Play each chord as two quarter notes.

3. Play two quarter notes per measure, each time starting with the root or fifth.

4. Play eighth notes on each beat followed by eighth rests.

5. Play eighth notes on each downbeat followed by the rest of the chord on the up-beat.

6. Break up the chord into 8th notes.

7. Break up each chord into two sets of 8th note triplets.

8. Break up each chord into 16th notes.

Part 2—Tunes and Styles

Country and Western music is based on folk styles of years past, especially sentimental ballads and fast hoedowns from the 19th century and even earlier. The next song began as a sailor's lament called *O, Bury Me Not in the Deep, Deep Sea* written in about 1850. The cowboy words are anonymous.

 Track 10

Bury Me Not on the Lone Prairie

Music by George N. Allen

Basic Melody

Variation 1 Sticks close to the melody

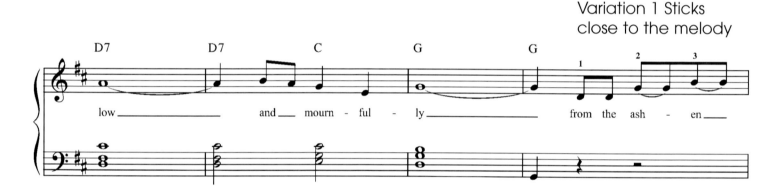

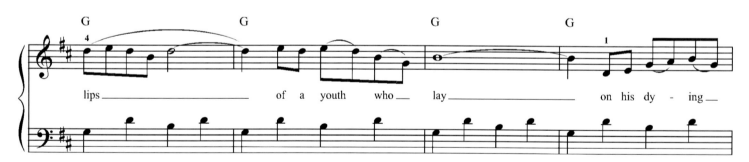

Left hand breaks up the chords into quarter notes

More variations on the next page

52

Variation 2.You may have noticed that this tune is based on the G pentatonic scale, G A B D E. This variation wanders further from the melody using that scale. The left hand breaks up the chords using open voicings. You may want to play the 8th notes unevenly (long-short, long-short) for a feeling often associated with cowboy songs.

Bury Me Not on the Lone Prairie (Cont.)

Variation 3 Ignores the melody; Continues in the pentatonic scale with grace notes.

Meanwhile, the left hand plays quarter notes based on the root and fifth (and occasionally the 3rd and 7th) of the chord.

Country and Western Styles (Cont.)

This old hobo song is ideal for building improvisations. The basic melody is a simple 12-bar tune which uses one new chord, E7. The notes in E7 are E G# B and D.

Railroad Bill

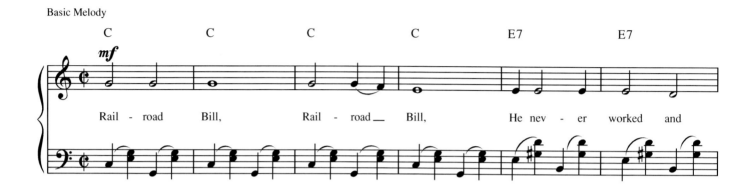

Rail - road Bill, Rail - road — Bill, He nev - er worked and

he nev - er will, and it s ride, ride, ride. ____

Variation 1 The melody is played an octave higher. This puts it into a brighter, more penetrating register. However, the sound can become a little thin, so we double it an octave lower.

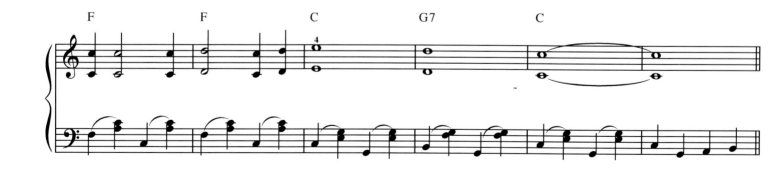

Variation 2. With the melody an octave higher, other chord tones are added below it. This produces a richer, fuller sound and makes your solo sound more complete. The lower octave is sometimes added to reinforce the sound. Also, since the melody is more complete, we can thin out the bass a little.

Railroad Bill

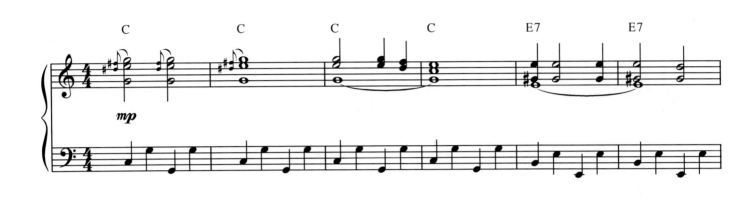

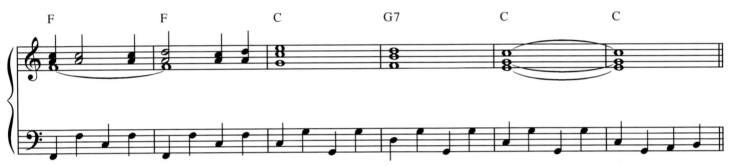

Variation 3. Breaks away from the melody and uses new rhythmic figures based on the chords. Notice the use of chromatic neighbor notes that add a little spice to the tune.

55

Country Waltz

Waltzes are a very popular country style in 3/4 time. All the techniques for improvising work, but now use only three beats in each measure. This cowboy classic has a simple but poignant melody.

Beautiful Brown Eyes

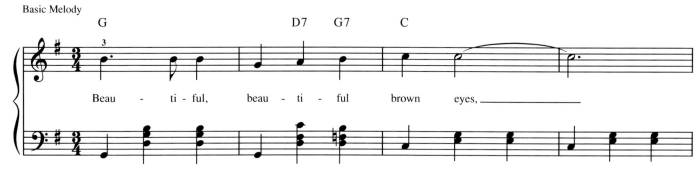

Left hand is a simple "oom-pa-pa" accompaniment

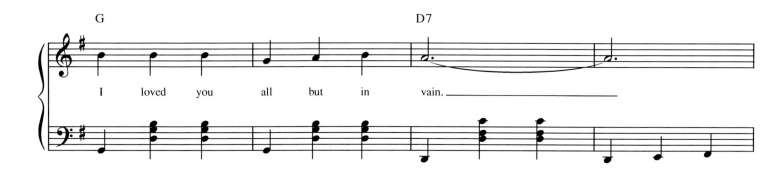

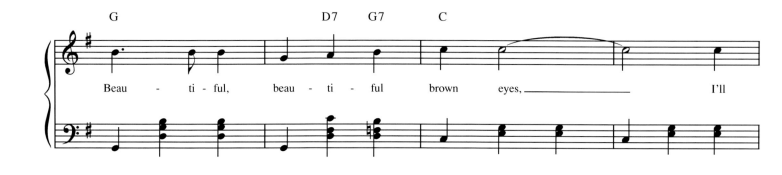

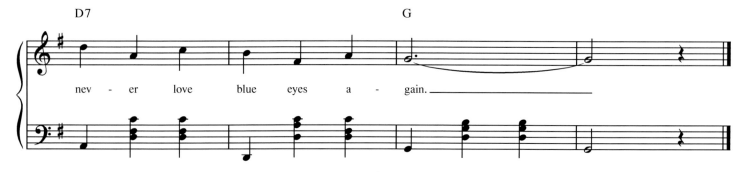

See the next two pages for variations

The first variation on this country waltz adds some harmony notes to the melody, but unlike Variation 2 of "Railroad Bill," adds the harmony *above* the melody. Try to bring out the melody note a little louder than the harmony.

Beautiful Brown Eyes

The last variation harmonizes the melody with 6ths and 3rds. But notice that when the melody is a chord tone, the harmony note is a chord tone. When the melody is a passing tone, the harmony is a passing tone. Fil-ins and runs avoid the dead spots in the melody (measures 4, 8, and 12).

Beautiful Brown Eyes

Bluegrass

Here's the first part of a traditional fiddle tune, *The Eighth of January*, which singer-song-writer Jimmy Driftwood used for his famous hit song *The Battle of New Orleans*. Old-time fiddle tunes can sometimes be adapted to the keyboard, especially ones like this that give you a chance to create many variations in different styles.

Track 11

The Eighth of January

For our first variation we have limited this solo to the same notes, but have sequenced them differently. When you have created a new solo and are uncertain whether it works with the chords of the original tune, have a friend play the chords while you lay down the solo. Or, tape the chords and play the solo over them.

The 2nd variation explores the lower notes in the key of D. A change of register—higher or lower—is always welcome in a series of variations, as the ear soon tires of hearing the same notes over and over.

Historical note: The 8th of January, 1815 was the date of General Andrew Jackson's great victory over the British near New Orleans.

The next variation uses figures that create the effect of syncopation (sin-co-PAY-shun). Ordinarily notes that occur on the down beats get a slight accent. When up-beat notes are accented, this effect is called syncopation. It's a very effective device in a series of variations as syncopation interrupts the smooth flow of the notes and surprises the ear.

The Eighth of January

The 4th variation moves both hands into a higher register. This achieves a much lighter type of sound which contrasts pleasantly with other lower variations.

Another variation in the upper register.

Our final variation shifts the melody to the left hand. The right hand plays the chords, accenting the 2nd and 4th beats of each measure.

Our final selection is an old murder ballad which has become a Bluegrass standard. It is written in the key of A, which means that F, C, and G are always sharped. The most important chords in the key of A are the I, IV, and V7: A=A C# E; D=D F# A; and E7=E G# B D. This song also uses the A7 (A C# E G) and E (E G# B) chords.

Banks of the Ohio

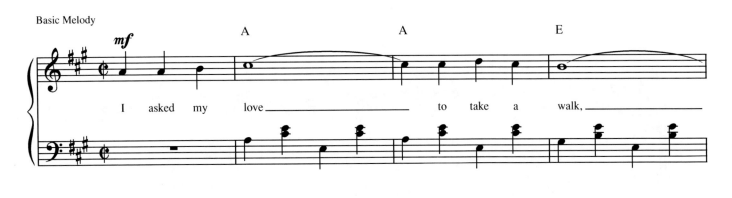

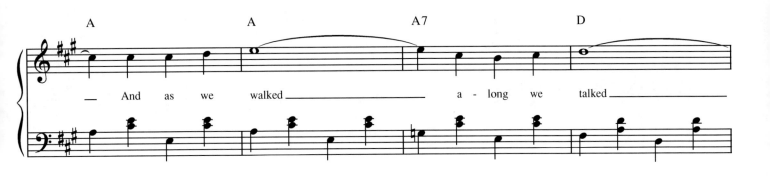

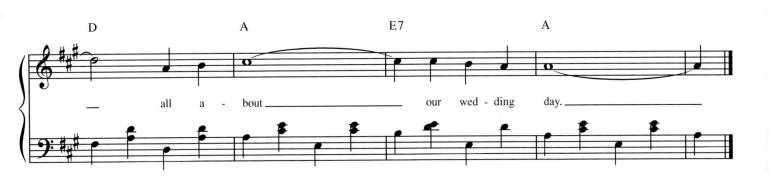

Chorus:
And only say that you'll be mine / In our home we'll happy be
Out beside where the waters flow / Down by the banks of the Ohio

Our first variation introduces a new technique. Take a look at the bass line. We have created a figure that sort of "walks along." If you analyze it in terms of the chords you find the following: Root, root an 8va higher, lower neighbor to the 3rd, the 3rd itself, and finally the 5th of the chord. This pattern is applied to all the chords in the song. We have also added a harmony part to the right-hand melody.

Banks of the Ohio

Our second variation makes use of a device called a pedal point or drone. A pedal point is a note that is repeated along with a melody note throughout a long section of a tune. The note can be repeated even when it is not part of the chord. Pedal points can appear below, above, or even some place in the middle of a melody. In the first eight and last three measures the note E is the pedal point; it is always above the melody note.

Banks of the Ohio

The eighth note triplet is a group of three eighth notes played in the time of two eighth notes, that is, one beat. This variation combines eighth note triplets with the pedal point from the previous page. This time, however, the pedal point is usually below the melody note.

Banks of the Ohio

Irish (Celtic) Music

Many Irish tunes are in rapid 6/8 time. Count in two groups of three 8th notes, with the 1st and 4th beats getting the accent: **1** 2 3 **4** 5 6. The first example is an old dance tune sometimes uses for the Virginia reel. Am7 (A minor seventh) is a new chord consisting of A C E and G. G/B means a G chord with B in the bass. G/D is a G chord with D in the bass.

The Irish Washerwoman

Although improvisations usually involve adding notes, sometimes a good effect can be obtained by simplifying a melody and reducing it to its essential notes. This is especially effective when dealing with a very busy melody like "The Irish Washerwoman." Notice how this version outlines the melody but with fewer notes. We have also moved Part 2 of the song up an octave to a brighter register.

The Irish Washerwoman

Irish jigs are often played at a medium tempo. One of their characteristics is the dotted 8th/16th rhythm which gives the jig a skipping, joyous feel. The chords are the I, IV, and V7 in the key of A minor: Am=A C E; Dm=D F A; E7= E G♯ B D.

Straight Jig

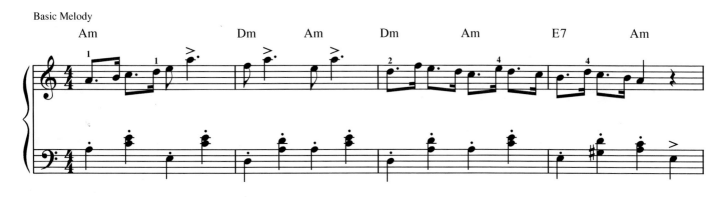

Our first variation adds an eighth note triplet figure to the basic rhythm. This is another typical jig rhythm.

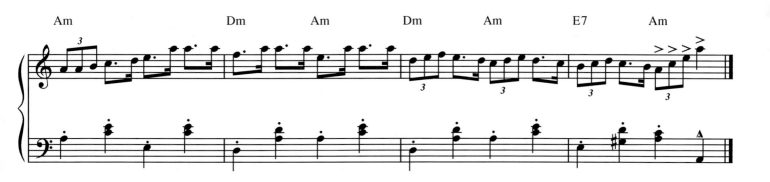

Our next variation consists of a steady stream of 8th note triplets. Because this figure occurs over and over again, the "3" over each group is omitted. But notice that the melody is still recognizable.

Straight Jig

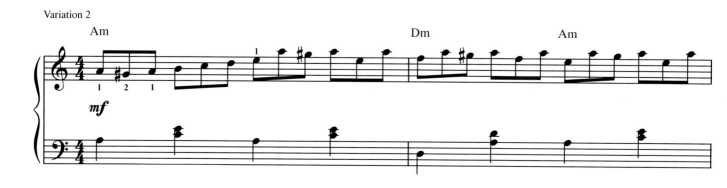

Our final variation steps up the rhythm to 16th notes. As usual, start slowly and gradually work your way up to tempo (about 120 bpm).

A famous Irish jig that makes liberal use of eighth note triplets and the dotted 8th/16th note figure, typical for this type of music.

Stack O' Barley

Irish Jig

Sometimes when you start with a good tune (like this one) the best thing you can do is just repeat it. To get some variety, however, play this variation an octave higher. We've also added a few typical embellishments.

Stack O' Barley

Irish Jig

71

Left-Hand Accompaniment Patterns in 6/8 Time (Slow to Medium Tempos)

When 6/8 is played at slower tempos such as "Greensleeves" or "Drink to Me Only with Thine Eyes," count in 6 with slight accents on the 1st and 4th beats: **1** 2 3 **4** 5 6. The following accompaniment patterns are appropriate for slower 6/8 tempos and are based on the I, IV, V7, I in the key of G: G, C, D7, G.

No. 1 Play each chord as an arpeggio (ar-PED-joe) (an Italian word that means "like a harp.")

Note: Usually arpeggios are played from bottom to top, but from top to bottom can work also.

Your call.

No. 2 Play a chord on each 8th note

(See section on 50s rock for more about this.)
No. 3 Combine bass note on 1 with chords on the other 8th notes

No. 4 Combine a bass note on 1 with chords on 2 and 3, and a bass run on 4, 5, and 6.

No. 5 Break up the chords into 8th notes.

No. 6 Another 8th note pattern

No. 7 Another way to break up the chords. This is more easily played using both hands, as for example accompanying a singer or soloist. (See Schubert's "Ave Maria.")

No. 8 Another two-hand pattern. Very effective for emotional ballads like "Nights in White Satin."

Left-Hand Accompaniment Patterns in 6/8 Time (Medium to Fast Tempos)

When 6/8 is played at faster tempos such as marches like *The Liberty Bell* or humorous songs like *Pop Goes the Weasel,* count in 2 with both beats accented. The following accompaniment patterns are appropriate for faster 6/8 tempos and again are based on the I, IV, V7, I in the key of G: G, C, D7, G.

No. 1 Play each chord as a dotted half note. This will get a sustained quality.

No. 2 Play two chords per measure. This is appropriate for marches or other tunes that require a steady beat.

No. 3 Play a steady stream of quarter and 8th notes. This can get a humorous "hump-ty dump-ty" sound.

No. 4 A variations of No. 3 that uses fuller chords.

No. 5 Still another variation of No. 3 that adds bass runs.

No. 6 A staccato pattern that uses full chords. Staccato (stuh-CAH-toe) is an Italian word that means "short."

No. 7 A variation of No. 5 that suggests the music of Spain. This can more easily be played with both hands.

O.K., now it's your turn. First, try adapting these patterns to other chords in other keys. Then, make up your own. Finally, find tunes in 6/8 that you like and see if you can create left-hand patterns that sound good.

American Folk Music

Like America itself, American folk music comes from many sources. Since the majority of the early settlers came from the British Isles, many of our most beautiful songs come from that culture. Although the definitive version of *Wildwood Flower* was recorded by The Carter Family in the 1920s, the original source is lost in history. Notice that the melody is based on a C major hexachord (six-note scale), C D E F G A; that is, just like the C major scale but avoiding the leading tone B.

Track 13

Wildwood Flower

74

This variation keeps the melody intact, but creates more interesting left-hand patterns.

Wildwood Flower

Although this pattern uses a passing tone, it still outlines the C major chord (C E G)

Our next variation ignores the melody with an almost constant stream of 8th notes. Although the melody is not played, the chords and number of measures are the same as in the basic melody. This type of playing should not be used until the melody is firmly fixed in your audience's mind. It is also very effective when played at the same time as the melody being played by a guitar, banjo, or fiddle.

Wildwood Flower

If you can get a friend to play the melody on page 74 on a second keyboard or other instrument, you can play this solo simultaneously with it!

76

Our final variation on *Wildwood Flower* keeps a steady stream of quarter notes going in the bass. The melody is almost intact, but a line under the melody that adds off-beat accents adds an exciting rhythmic drive similar to what guitar players call "Travis picking." This technique is particularly effective when the melody has many sustained notes…whole notes, halves, and quarters.

Wildwood Flower

Many folk songs are in 3/4 time such as this typical example. Besides the I, IV, and V7 chords in the key of C (C, F, and G7) you'll need Am=A C E, Em=E G B, and Dm=D F A.

Sweet Betsy from Pike

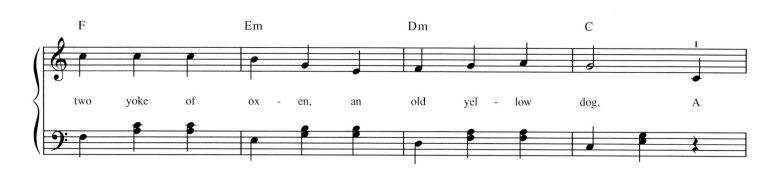

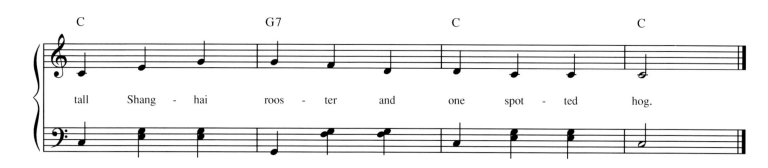

Suggestion: Review the accompaniment patterns on page 50. See if you can incorporate them into this arrangement.

Our first variation mixes runs of 8th notes with partial or full chords. Notice that in this style of playing it generally sounds better to avoid chromatic notes. Pay particular attention to the chord sequence in measures 10–13 which is played in the upper positions.

Sweet Betsy from Pike

Here again, refer to page 50 for other ways of playing the left hand.

Our last variation takes the melody up an octave and adds a staccato to many notes. This gives a light, airy feeling very suitable to humorous songs like this.

Sweet Betsy from Pike

Latin-American and Caribbean Music

Ever since the tango emerged from the slums of Buenos Aires in the 1880s, Latin-American and Caribbean music has played a more and more important role in American culture. By the early 1900s the tango had become an American and international craze. In the 1920s bandleader Xavier Cugat introduced Americans to the rhumba, a Cuban dance, and soon there followed other dances such as the samba and bossa nova (Brazil), bolero, cha-cha-cha, conga, and mambo (Cuba), beguine (Martinique), merengue (Dominican Republic), ska and reggae (Jamaica), calypso (Trinidad), and most recently, "reggaeton" (Mexico).

When you see a Latin band performing, who's the most important member? Is it trumpet player reaching for high notes? The flutist playing exciting countermelodies? The pianist with his runs and chords? The sexy singer? The rhythm section consisting of from one to five players? No, none of these. The key member of the band bangs together two hollow sticks called claves (CLAH-vays), and the penetrating click they produce is the reference point for every other member of the orchestra as they play their intricate rhythms and syncopated counter-rhythms.

Example 79B.1. The basic clave beat consists of a two-bar figure in 4/4 time:

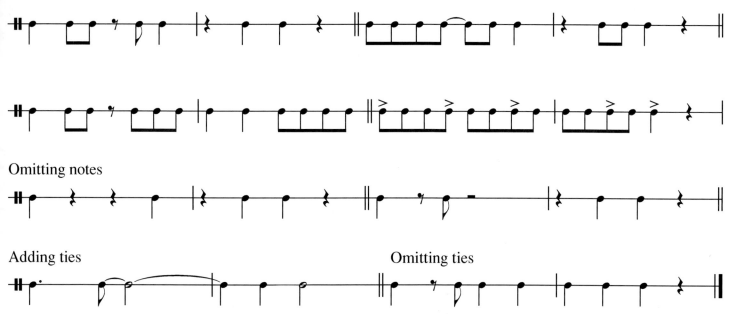

Some American musicians like to use the phrase "shave, hair-cut, two bits" to remember the rhythm. Or, you may want to count it out as indicated. Make sure you understand this rhythm before tackling the Latin-American improvisations that follow. When you improvise in this style, keep in mind that what you play will sound more authentically Latin if its rhythms conform to the clave beat—or one of its variations—than if it doesn't. See the examples below.

Example 79B.2.

Adding notes to the basic beat

Omitting notes

Adding ties   **Omitting ties**

Important: Although most Latin and Caribbean music is based on the clave beat described above, some is not. Notable exceptions are bossa nova, ska, reggae, and "reggaeton."

Note: In a book this size we can only give you a taste of various Latin and Caribbean rhythms which could easily fill a book by themselves.

The rhumba (ROOM-bah) is a Cuban dance that's still very popular in the U.S. The bass line is typical and notice that the melody conforms fairly closely to the clave beat. The tempo is fast (about 192 bpm), so keep your improvs simple. The chords are Gm=G Bb D, D7=D F# A C, Bb=Bb D F, F7=F A C Eb, and D=D F# A.

Rhumba Typico

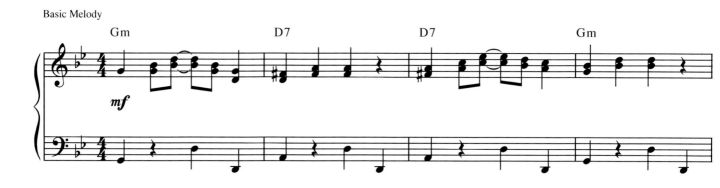

Here's one variation of endless possibilities. It's typical for the piano to play in octaves, but if you have trouble executing this passage, just play the upper notes.

The cha-cha-cha, or cha-cha as it's often called, was popularized in Cuba. It's played more slowly than a rhumba, about 120bpm. We'll give you a short example harmonized in block chords, a technique that works well in the key of C so that all the chords are on the white keys. Especially notice the bass line which gives the cha-cha its flavor.

Takin' a Chance on the Cha-Cha

This is a typical improv. It has a double-time feel, but keeps the bass line "cha-cha-cha" rhythm intact (in the last measure).

The bolero (bo-LAY-ro), another Cuban dance, is usually played at a moderate tempo, about 96 bpm. It features beautiful melodies, rich chords, and a rhythm that makes it one of the most popular Latin dances in America. Many American pop tunes can be—and often are—played as boleros. This example uses the chords Dm=D F A, E7=E G♯ B D, and A7=A C♯ E G, the I, II, and V7 chords in the key of D minor.

Moon Over Havana

Our sample variation takes the melody up the octave and doubles it at octave below. Also notice the runs in bars 3 and 4, and 7 and 8 that fill in the "dead spots" in the melody.

84

The mambo (MOM-bo) is an exciting Cuban dance that somewhat resembles the rhumba. It's also played rather fast and features a lot of syncopation (accented off-beats). A few decades ago the mambo took America by storm and it's still popular where Latin music is played. This arrangement uses four-part block chords. Easy to play because they're all on the white keys and the hand position remains the same. Also notice that this figure, although fairly complicated, conforms quite closely to the clave beat (see accents).

Momma's Mambo

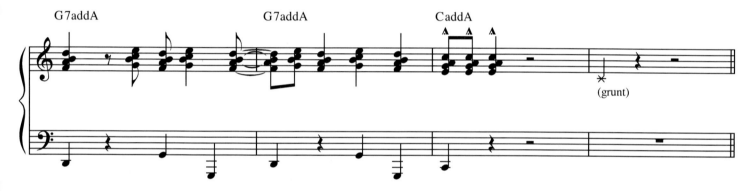

A typical improv creates a syncopated line played in octaves, as below.

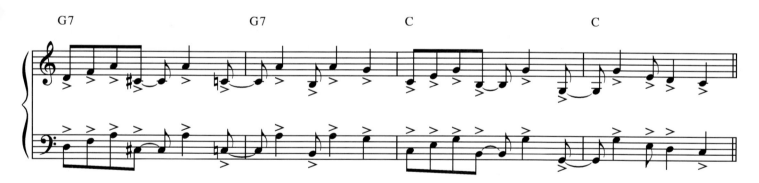

Or perhaps a repeated rhythmic figure. (But keep the clave beat in mind!)

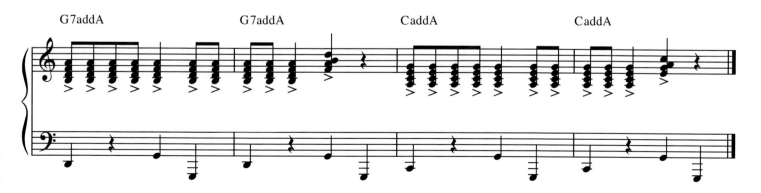

The meringue (meh-REN-gay) comes from the Dominican Republic, but is very popular in the States. It is played at a very bright tempo, with the half notes going by at about 120 bpm. The harmony is simple. The melody conforms closely to the clave beat and has a characteristic four-8th note run leading into each two-bar phrase. Because the tempo is so fast, keep your improv fairly simple and closely related to the clave beat. New chord: G+ (G augmented)=G B D♯.

Midnight Merengue

The last section, called the montuno, allows you or musicians you're playing with to improvise freely over a repeated rhythmic figure as in this example. The four-bar figure is repeated over and over while various musicians create their improvs. Since the harmony is very simple (the I and V7 chords in the key of C) you can use all the techniques you've learned, especially running the C major scale, diatonic and chromatic passing tones and neighbor notes, block chords, etc. If you have enough technique, double your melody in octaves. Generally, after playing the montuno for a while the entire melody is repeated.

The beguine (beh-GEEN) is perhaps the most popular Latin-American rhythm in America. Starting with Cole Porter's *Begin the Beguine* in the early 1930's, this rhythm has been the basis for dozens of great standards. The melody should always predominate, and the rhythm is maintained throughout. Here's an example of how a non-Latin melody from Puccini's opera *Madama Butterfly* can be adapted to the beguine rhythm.

Un Bel Di

Giacomo Puccini

88

Limitations of space prevent us from giving longer samples of other Latin music, but here are some four-measure examples that will point you in the right direction.

Calypso (kuh-LIP-so) is really guitar based folk music, but if asked to play something in this rhythm, keep the chords very simple (usually the I, IV, and V7) and make sure the vocalist can be understood clearly.

The conga (CONG-ah) is a Cuban dance that has a characteristic "one-two-three-kick" rhythm. It is often played at social functions where the participants form a long line and snake their way around the dance floor. The main thing is to accent the "kick" every two measures. Notice that the clave beat is reversed in this rhythm.

The tango (TANG-o) comes from Argentina and, strictly speaking, uses an accordion-like instrument called the bandoneon rather than a piano. You might have one on your keyboard. The most important thing about the rhythm is the accented 4th and 1st beats of the bar as in this example. The tempo is a brisk 120 beats per minute. The clave is not used.

The samba (SAHM-ba) comes from Brazil. In its native country the samba is played dozens of different ways, but in the States it usually sounds like this: (Clave is usually not used, but if it is used is often reversed as in this example).

Ragtime

Some time after the Civil War African-American pianists living in the Southwest started playing in a syncopated style they called "ragging the time." This was soon shortened to "ragtime," and by 1900 the music became an international craze. Although improvisation is not a particularly important part of ragtime, this example will show you a few possibilities. The first tune dates from 1909 and is in two parts, the first in A minor and the second in F major. See pages 92 and 93 for variations.

Temptation Rag

Track 15

Original Melody

Henry Lodge

90

This variation makes use of various embellishments, octave doublings, and other techniques you have learned. However, when playing ragtime it's usually best to leave the melody unchanged.

Temptation Rag

Henry Lodge

White Gospel

White gospel is a very emotional type of music, often with a mournful quality, especially popular in the South. All the techniques you have applied to folk and bluegrass may be used. We've already added harmony notes and a few bass runs.

Rhythmically, the 1st and 3rd beats of the measure are accented as opposed to Black gospel (which see).

 Track 16

Will the Circle Be Unbroken

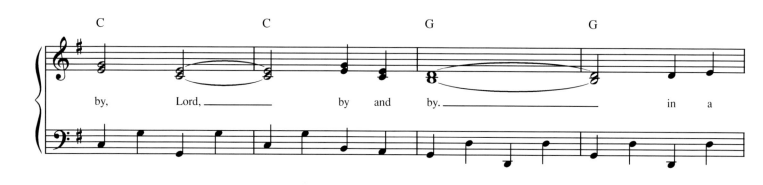

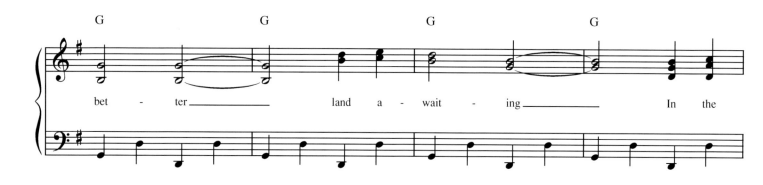

This variation makes use of techniques you've already dealt with. The tremolo or shake in measure 24 is played by keeping the hand stiff and rapidly shaking the wrist.

Black Gospel

Like White gospel, Black gospel is a highly emotional music with a strong rhythmic feel. Unlike White gospel, however, the accents fall on the 2nd and 4th beats of the measure. Eighth notes tend to be played more freely—long-short—rather than evenly. This famous gospel song is based on an E minor pentatonic scale: E G A B D. Syncopation is an important feature of this music. Count carefully as indicated.

Wade in the Water

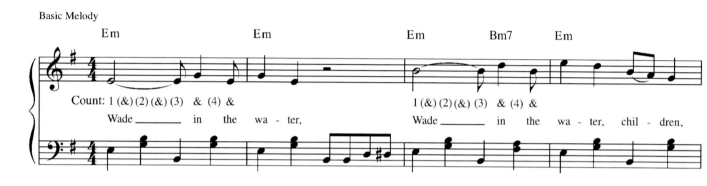

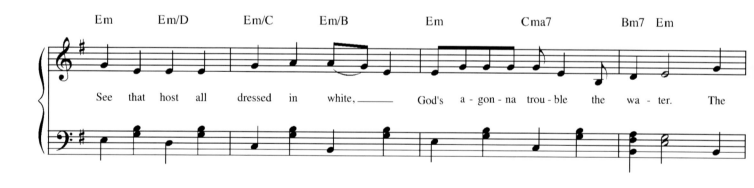

96

One characteristic of African-American music is the use of "blue notes." Ordinarily these are the lowered 7th, lowered 3rd, and sometimes lowered 5th of a major scale. Since the pentatonic scale E G A B D already has the 3rd (G) and 7th (D) lowered, the only accidental needed is B♭, the lowered 5th.

Wade in the Water

The Blues

Modern blues are usually based on a 12-bar series of chords called "the blues progression." Musicians sometimes use Roman numerals to refer to chords in a key. For example in the key of C the I chord is C major, the IV is F major, and the V7 chord is G7. The basic blues progression consists of one measure each of the following chords: I I I I7 IV7 IV7 I I V7 V7 I I (V7). Of course, there are hundreds of variations on this basic progression, but the above sequence will be useful in most situations.

Track 17

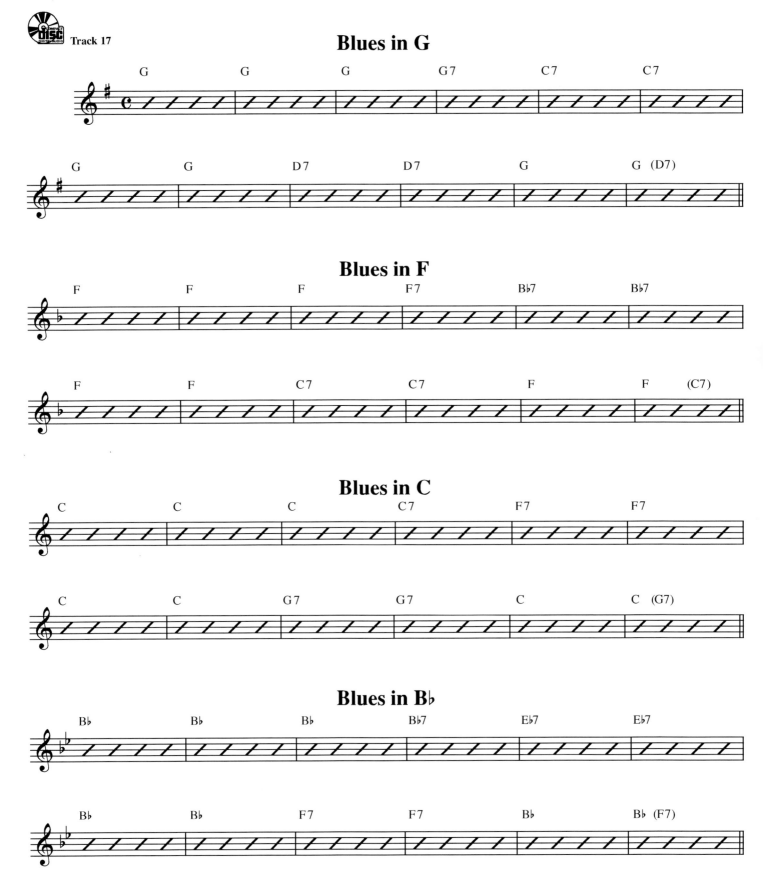

One of the things that makes the blues so interesting is the tension between the notes in the blues scale with the notes in the accompanying chords. For example, the G blues scale uses a B♭ while the accompanying chord (G7) uses a B natural. The best thing about blues scales is that any note you play will sound good against the chords. Here are four blues scales in the most used keys.

The G Blues Scale

Notice the flatted 3rd, the flatted 7th, and the 5th, which can be flat or natural.

The F Blues Scale

The C Blues Scale

The B♭ Blues Scale

99

Piano Blues

Compared to blues guitar work, playing the blues on piano is a bit of a challenge. As previously mentioned, one of the main characteristics of the blues is the use of "blue notes," the lowered third, seventh, and sometimes fifth of the major scale. For example, the C major scale contains the notes C D E F G A B and C. In blues playing it is customary to play the third and seventh notes as E♭ and B♭ respectively. The G is sometimes played as G♭ also. Actually the first pitch is between an E and an E♭. If you have an electronic keyboard you can use the pitch bend wheel to bend the note from an E♭ up about a quarter tone to not quite an E natural. On acoustic piano you can either play the E and E♭ notes consecutively or both together in what's sometimes called a "smash."

In blues playing major chords and seventh chords are interchangeable, so in the key of C you might play a C7 (C E G B♭) in place of a C, or an F7 (F A C E♭) in place of an F. Notice that the seventh of each chord (B♭ and E♭) are the two main blue notes in the C scale.

Below is a blues chord progression. For now you won't need to play any individual notes with the right hand. Just play the chords as written, with the left hand playing the bass clef notes and the right hand playing the notes in the treble clef.

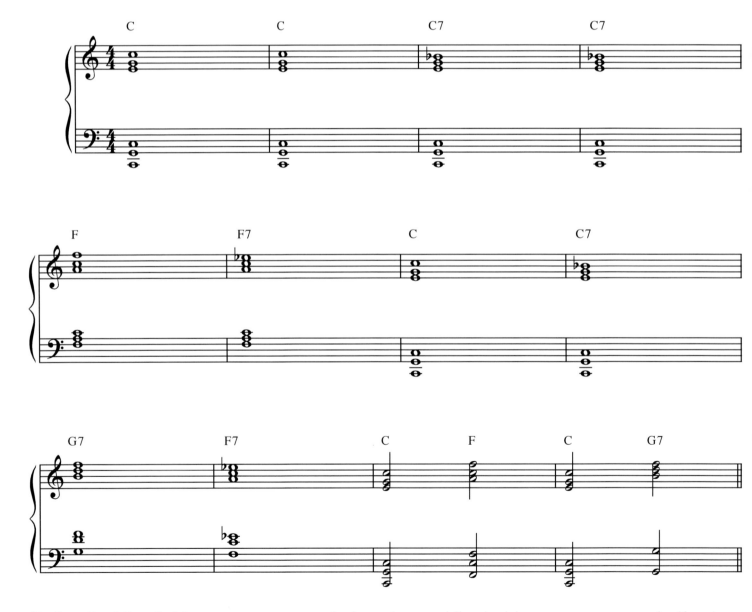

Notice that the first ten measures use whole notes and the last two measures use half notes. This last chord progression C F C G7 is called a "turnaround." It often appears at the end of a blues chorus to lead the chords back to the beginning for another chorus.

Blues All Alone

Here's a simple blues tune that makes use of the progression on the previous page. Notice the use of blue notes in the melody. Also notice the use of chord inversions. These are chords in which the root is not the lowest note. For example, in measures 1-6 the chords are in root position (the root is the lowest note). In measures 7-12 the chords are inverted. Meas. 7-8 the C chords have a G (the 5th) in the bass. In meas. 8-9 the G and F chords have the 7th in the bass, and so on. Chord inversions give you variations in sound as well as making it easier to move from one chord to the next.

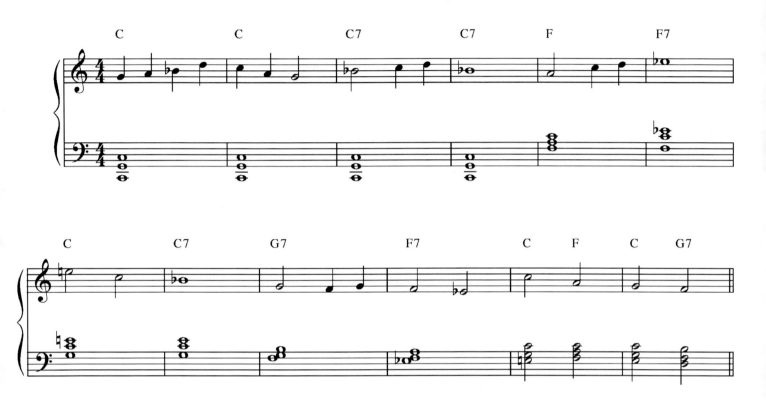

In this variation the right hand remains the same. The left hand plays mostly arpeggio figures to give forward motion to the piece.

101

This variation uses two new devices. In the right hand, the shake is a commonly used effect in the blues. Just rapidly alternate between the two (or more) written notes. Meanwhile, the left hand plays a more rhythmic version of the chord arpeggios.

Let's take a look at the last three chords in the left hand. These wide-spaced intervals are called 10ths (from F through G A B C D E F G to A is ten notes). For players with large hands this is an economical way to produce full-sounding chords with only two notes. Many great jazz and blues pianists have used this effect. On the next page we'll use a series of 10ths to demonstrate how 10ths can be used to keep a chord progression moving. If you can't reach the 10ths, you can play the lower note with the 5th finger and quickly skip to the upper note with the thumb while holding the chord with the sustain pedal.

Blues Variation No. 2

Of course, the blues could be a subject that would fill many books, so we'll have to leave you with a few suggestions on how to vary the bass on a C chord. You can easily adapt them to other chords...

Open 5ths with added 3rd, both flat and natural.   Open 5ths with added neighbor notes.

Rock and Roll

The chord progression C Am Dm7 (or F) G7—sometimes called the I VI II (or IV) V progression—is found in many 50s pop and rock songs including "Why Must I Be a Teenager in Love," "Heart and Soul," "26 Miles," "Blue Moon," and many others. Here are five ways to play this progression.

1. The basic progression with chords in the right hand and bass notes in the left.

Track 18

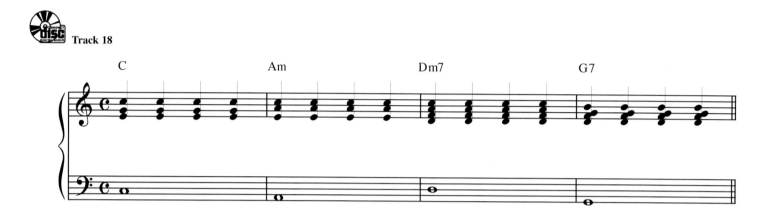

2. Triplets in the r.h. and quarter notes in the l.h. Typical of "doo-wop" ballads from the 50s and 60s. Better when the tempo is rather slow.

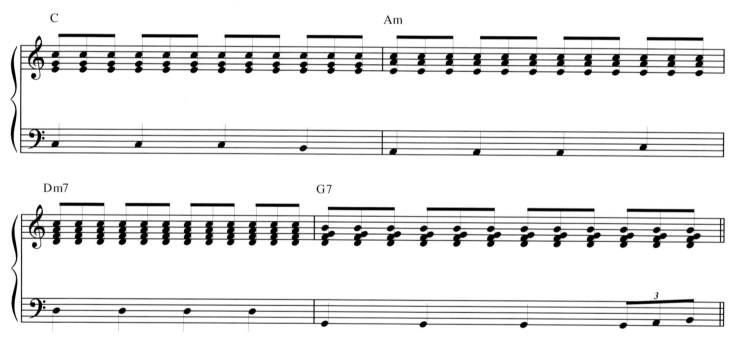

3. Quarter notes in the r.h. and triplet arpeggios in the l.h. Good for doo-wop ballads at slow tempos.

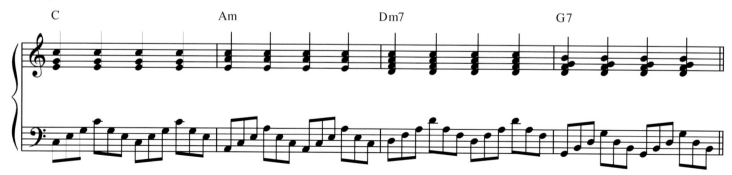

4. "Hump-ty dump-ty" rhythm. Good for medium tempo ballads such as *Heart and Soul*.

5. Good for faster tempos. Make sure to accent the second beat of each measure.

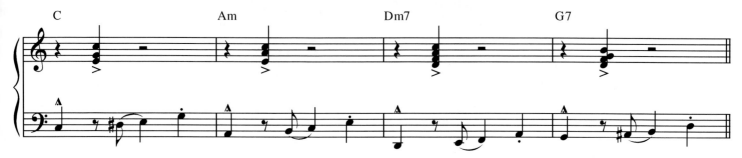

6. Good for fast, bluesy tempos

7. Good for fast rock tunes.

We could go on for pages more, but we hope you get the idea. You can also expand these seven rhythms like this:

1. Substitute F for Dm7. Many rock tunes use the IV chord instead of the II7

2. Transpose these rhythms to other keys, especially those most used in rock, G, F, D, A, and E.

3. Play the patterns twice as fast. That is, have each chord last for two beats instead of four.

4. Adapt these rhythms to your favorite rock tunes.

5. Adapt these patterns to different progressions, especially the blues progressions you learned in the previous section.

Our final versions of the I VI II V progression have a double-time feel sometimes called "boogaloo." The 4/4 measures are felt as eight even beats to the bar; that is, each eighth note gets a beat. Famous records that have this feel are The Beatle's *Let It Be,* and The BeeGees *Stayin' Alive.* These examples are based on the I VI IV V7 progression in the key G.

In general it always works to use diatonic (in the scale) notes when improvising in this style. Half step grace notes from below can also be used, but avoid too many chromatic (not in the scale) notes, as these are more fitting for avant garde jazz tunes than for rock.

Country and Folk Rock

Folk-rock differs from both folk and rock in that the chord progressions are usually more sophisticated, but all the techniques you learned in those two styles will work here. We'll give you a short example with a variation designed to suggest the feel of The Eagles' famous *Hotel California.* You should be familiar with all the chords used, but we'll review them just the same: Am=A C E; E7=E G# B D; G=G B D; D=D F# A; F=F A C; A=A C# E.

Nevada Motels

This variation ignores the melody and plays a 3+3+2 eighth note figure that suggests syncopation because some of the accents fall on the up-beats. Notice that because the right hand is rhythmically more complex, the left hand reverts to a simple quarter note pattern.

Odd meters

So far in this book we have dealt with meters that are common in Western popular music, 2/4, 3/4, 6/8, and especially 4/4 and cut time. In many parts of the world it's common to play music in odd meters such as 5/4 or 7/8. Odd meters are interesting because they produce asymmetrical measures. In 4/4 we hear two halves of a measure, each like a measure of 2/4. In 6/8, the two halves contain three 8th notes each. But in an odd meter such as 5/4, one half of the measure contains three quarter notes; the other half only two.

The key to counting odd meters is to break them down into smaller units. For example, one measure of 5/4 can be thought of as a measure of 3/4 followed by a measure of 2/4. Or, one measure of 2/4 followed by a measure of 3/4.

Example 107B.1.

Similarly, a measure of 7/8 is usually counted as a measure of 3/8 followed by a measure of 2/4 (4/8) although it can be counted 2/8+3/8+2/8 or 2/4+3/8. The Greeks are particularly fond of 7/8, and their folk music is full of examples of this meter.

Example 107B.2.

Although in Western music 9/8 is usually counted as three groups of three 8th notes, in Greece and the near East it is often played as 2/8+2/8+2/8+3/8.

Example 107B.3.

Here is a chart that shows how to count many odd meters, although we wish to stress that other combinations are possible, and that the ones here are only the most common ways of counting them.

5/2, 5/4, or 5/8: 3+2 or 2+3. Counting in an even five beats to the measure is rare but can be found in the slow movement of Tchaikovsky's 4th symphony. 5/2 is very unusual, but was used in a few spots by Samuel Barber in his famous "Adagio for Strings."

6/4 or 6/8: Almost always counted in two groups of three, but listen to the song "America" from Leonard Bernstein's "West Side Story" for 6/8 counted alternately in two groups of three followed by three groups of two.

7/4 or 7/8: see above

9/8: see above

10/8: Usually counted 3+2+2+3. Very common in Romanian folk music.

11/8: 3+2+3+3, 3+3+3+2, or 3+2+2+2+2.

Even more elaborate rhythms are possible, but just remember to break them down into groups of 3 and 2.

In this example 5/4 is sometimes counted 3+2 and sometimes 2+3.

Track 19

Five Times Four

Basic Melody

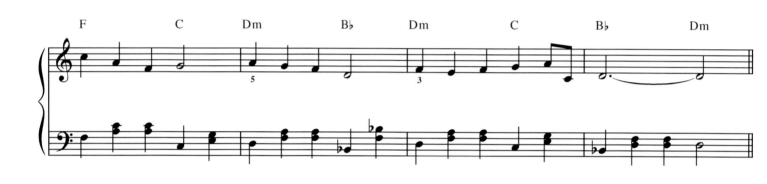

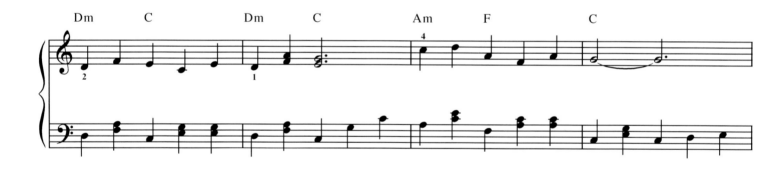

Five Times Four

111

The next piece is in 7/8 counted 1 2 3 1 2 1 2. It is in the mixolydian mode, which is identical to the key of G but with an F natural instead of an F♯. The Bela of the title refers to the great 20th century Hungarian composer Bela Bartók who often used odd meters in his compositions.

The Other Bela

Our first variation simplifies the melody but adds more motion in the left hand.

112

Our second variation breaks up the chords very rhythmically. This variation can also be used as an accompaniment to the melody. Notice the use of the low G pedal point in the first eight measures and the C pedal point in the last eight measures…

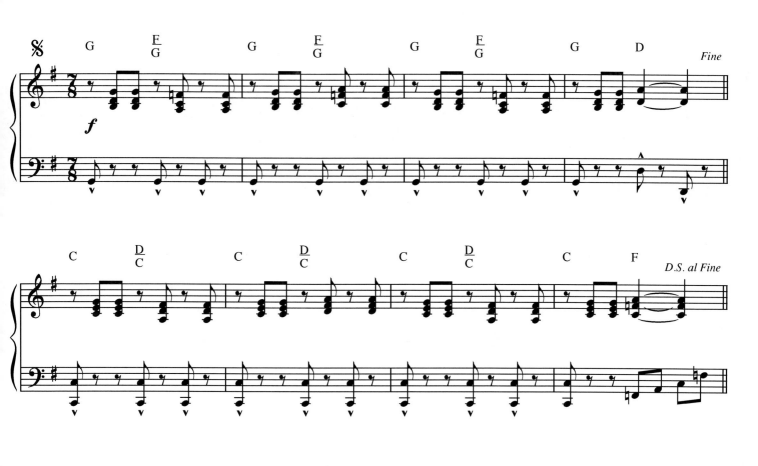

Our final variation combines chords with rapid single-note passages.

Although 9/8 time is usually counted in three groups of three 8th notes, the example below illustrates that other combinations are possible. This 9/8 is counted 1 2 1 2 1 2 1 2 3. Many Greek folk songs and dances are written in this meter. Here's a four-bar fragment and three variations on it.

Odyssey in 9/8

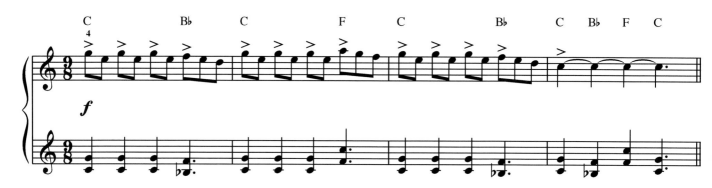

Var. 1 Simplified version of melody with more motion in the left hand.

Var. 2 Chords broken up rhythmically

Var. 3. A higher version with a very percussive sound.

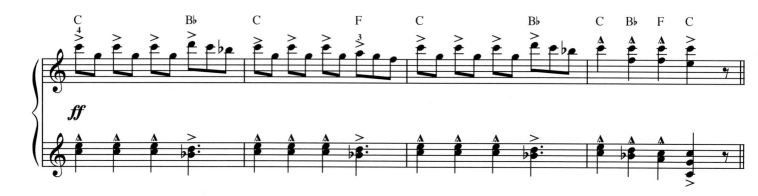

Exotic Scales

Certain scales have such a distinctive sound that you can use them to suggest a particular mood or culture. Although it's beyond the scope of this book to give you all of them (there are hundreds!) we'll give you a taste of the most useful ones.

The Whole Tone Scale
As the name suggests, this scale has the interval of a whole tone between each step. It's often used to suggest a dreamlike state, either in single notes or combined into chords.

Whole Tone Scale on D

Whole Tone Scale on E♭

A few things to remember about whole tone scales:

1. Because the scales have no real tonal center, the accidentals can be spelled with sharps or flats, depending on the surrounding music.

2. Because the scales consist only of whole steps (unlike major and minor scales which consist of half steps and whole steps) any note in the scale can serve as the key note.

3. The above two scales are the only possible whole tone scales.

Where to use the whole tone scale
You won't find many places to use this scale unless you're into avant garde jazz or other cutting-edge sounds. If the accompanying chord belongs to one of the whole tone scales you can use improvisations from the scale. For example, if the accompanying chord is C+ (C augmented), the notes in the chord are C E G♯, all of which belong to the D whole tone scale. You can then use that scale to create your improv.

Suggestion: Make up your own improvisation based on one or both of the whole tone scales.

A word of caution: Because of so many similar intervals (whole steps), the ear soon grows tired of this sound, so use it sparingly.

Klezmer Music

Klezmer music developed in central Europe hundreds of years ago. Itinerant Jewish musicians wandered through the countryside playing their music for a bare subsistence. During the early period of klezmer they absorbed influences from traditional Hassidic tunes, Turkish, Hungarian, Romanian and other folk songs. When they came to America starting in about 1880, they were influenced by what they heard, and in the 1920s were strongly influenced by jazz. Today there is a great resurgence in klezmer music which is featured by such modern groups as "The Klezmer Conservatory Band" and "The Klezmatics."

One of the things that makes this music so interesting is the use of exotic scales, one of which is called "Misherabach." This scale resembles the Dorian mode, but has a raised fourth step. It is usually written with a key signature of no sharps or flats with the fourth step (G) sharped whenever it occurs.

Misherabach

Track 20

Chosen Kalle Mazel Tov

Jewish Wedding Song

This variation makes use of typical devices of klezmer music especially grace notes, trills and scale runs. Notice that all the added notes belong to the scale Misherabach.

Chosen Kalle Mazel Tov

Many Klezmer tunes are in the harmonic minor. However, you'll notice that in the first two sections of this famous tune the tonal center is actually D, not G. It's only in Part 3 (next page) that the song arrives at the G minor tonality.

Havah Nagilah

Traditional Jewish Dance

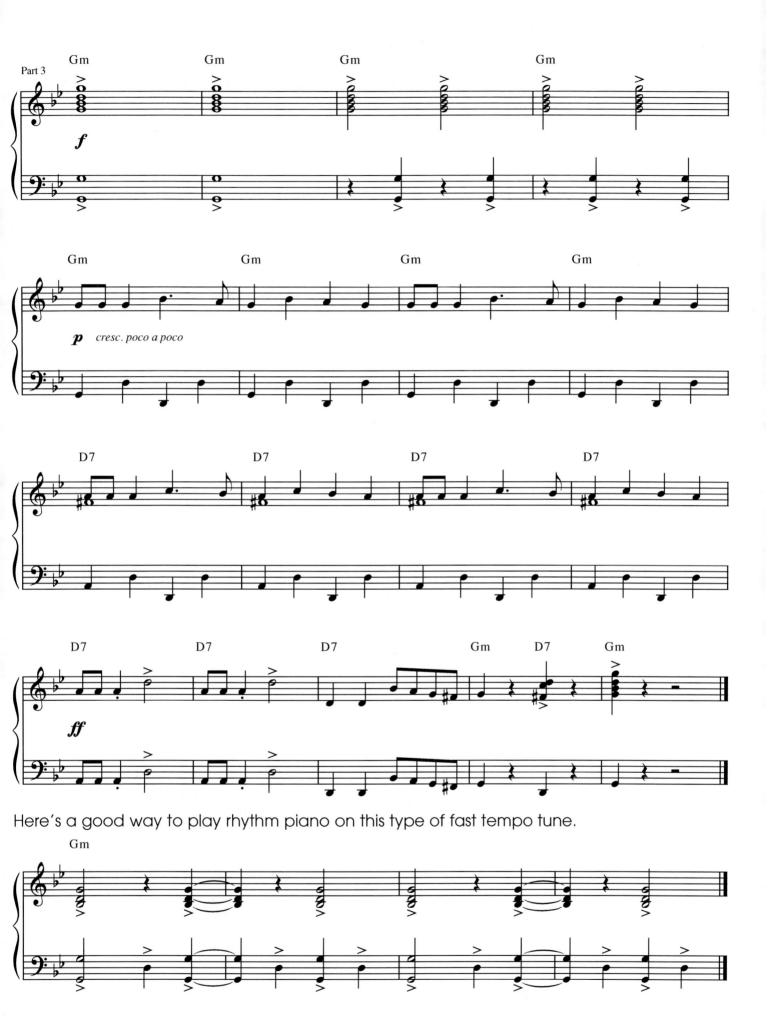

Here's a good way to play rhythm piano on this type of fast tempo tune.

Exotic Scales (Cont.)

A scale called "Fraigish" is a popular one in klezmer music. It is also used in Greek music especially in the famous song "Misirlou" (popular with both Greek and Jewish audiences). It is based on D, usually written with a two sharp key signature with the rest of the accidentals written in where needed. Notice the curious mixture of sharps and flats in the same scale. We've added some embellishments, but feel free to add your own.

Fraigish or Greek Scale

Goodbye to Piraeus

120

Gypsies began to arrive in Europe in about the 15th century. They brought with them a long tradition that incorporated many musical elements including some from North India, their ancestral home. Once in Europe they absorbed many elements from those musics, especially those from Spain and Hungary. This is one of the many exotic scales that Gypsies use in their folk music. It resembles a D harmonic minor scale, but with the fourth (G) raised a half step to G#.

Gypsy Scale

Gypsy Fantasy

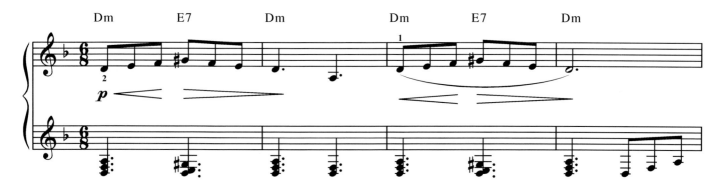

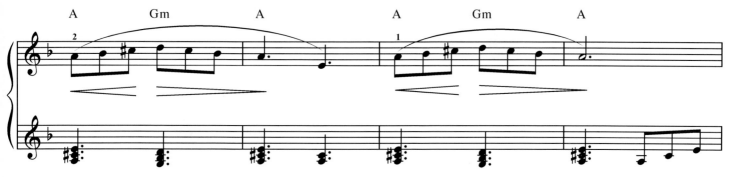

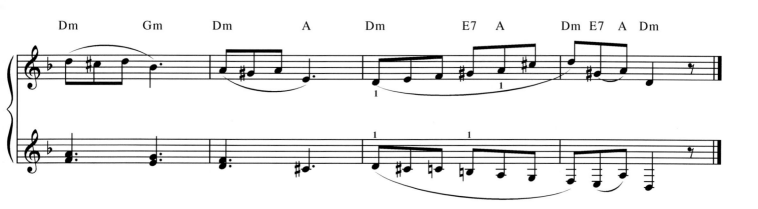

The Japanese culture is one of the world's richest in terms of poetry, art, and music, so we can only scratch the surface here. One of the scales used in much of Japanese folk music is a pentatonic scale on D. It resembles a D natural minor scale but with the fourth step (G) and the seventh step (C) omitted.

Japanese Pentatonic Scale

Traditionally, Japanese melodies are not harmonized, but when playing Westernized versions it is appropriate to add chords as in the example below.

The Geisha's Lament

122

The Chinese culture is one of the world's oldest. Much Chinese folk music is based on the pentatonic scale C E♭ F G B♭ as in the example below. Keep your variations to the pentatonic scale although chromatic embellishments may be used.

The Golden Bell

Note: Traditionally, Chinese melodies are not harmonized but chords may be added as above for a more Westernized sound.

Cajun Music

The Cajuns were French colonists who were exiled from Acadia (Nova Scotia) during wars with the British in the 18th century. The word "Cajun" itself is a corruption of "Acadian." Now living in Southern Lousiana, the Cajuns have developed a unique sound, an interesting blend of country fiddle and accordion with lots of slides and swoops (all sung in an 18th century French dialect). Although the piano is not a particularly important part of Cajun music, perhaps you have an accordion stop on your keyboard. We'll give you a taste of two famous tunes.

This piece is in two eight-bar sections, each of which is repeated.

Track 21

Joli Blon
(Pretty Blond)

Basic Melody

When playing variations, it's probably best to stick fairly close to the melody, using single and double grace notes, and sliding up into a melody note. Adding harmony notes, passing tones, and neighbor notes also work well, but we advise you to use diatonic (in the scale) rather than chromatic notes.

124

Along with waltzes such as the one the previous page, a bright two-step rhythm is also very popular in Cajun circles. This traditional tune bears more than a passing resemblance to *Oh Susannah*. We'll give you the basic melody and one variation. Then create your own.

J'ete Au Bal
(At the Ball)

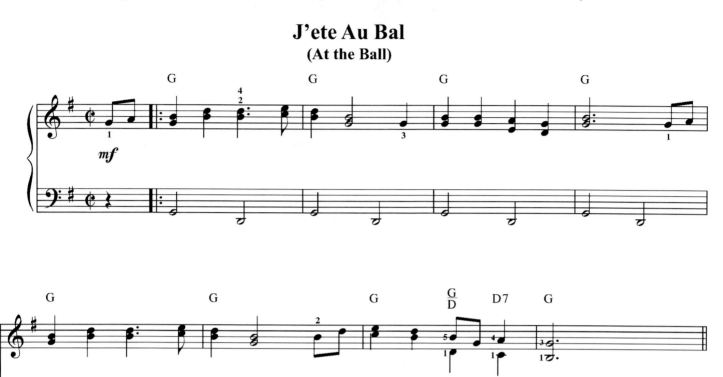

Our variation is in typical Cajun style. Here again, if you have an accordion attachment on your keyboard, use it.

Brazilian Music-Bossa Nova

It's entirely possible that Brazil has more talented musicians per square mile than any other country in the world. At least it seems that way if you go to Rio, Sao Paulo, or any other big city there. Every street has some-one standing on the corner making music—even if it's only scraping on a matchbox or strumming on a cigar box with rubber bands across it. Since the native language of Brazil is Portuguese, it can't be considered a Latin-American country, but in some ways Brazilian music does resemble the music of those countries.

We've already mentioned the samba in an earlier section. The other Brazilian dance that's very popular in the States is the bossa nova (new wave) which, since the groundbreaking recordings by jazz great Stan Getz in the 60s, has played an important part on the American music scene. The harmony has been greatly influenced by American jazz, especially from the be-bop era. The chords are full of half-diminished, 7ths with flat 5ths or sharp 5ths, major 7ths, major 9ths, minor 9ths, and other altered and extended chords typical of modern American jazz. The following chart identifies 7ths, major 7ths, 9ths, 11ths, and 13ths. Just take the basic triad (three-note chord) and add the appropriate additional notes. For example, to find a C major 9th, start with a C major chord (C E G and add the major 7th (B) and the major 9th (D). To find a C minor 11th chord, start with a C minor (C E♭ G) and add the minor 7th (B♭), 9th (D) and 11th (F). Since five-and six-note chords can get a little difficult to play, some notes are usually omitted, especially the 5th and/or root of the chord.

Root	Minor 7th	Major 7th	Ninth	Eleventh	Thirteenth
C	B♭	B	D	F	A
C♯	B	B♯	D♯	F♯	A♯
D♭	C♭	C	E♭	G♭	B♭
D	C	C♯	E	G	B
E♭	D♭	D	F	A♭	C
E	D	D♯	F♯	A	C♯
F	E♭	E	G	B♭	D
F♯	E	E♯	G♯	B	D♯
G♭	F♭	F	A♭	C♭	E♭
G	F	F♯	A	C	E
A♭	G♭	G	B♭	D♭	F
A	G	G♯	B	D	F♯
B♭	A♭	A	C	E♭	G
B	A	A♯	C♯	E	G♯
C♭	B♭	B♭	D♭	F♭	A♭

If you studied the section on Latin-American music (page 79-87) you already know how important the clave beat is. A similar situation exists with the clave beat in the bossa nova, except that a subtle—but very important—change has been made in it. In the bossa nova, the clave beat consists of two measures; the second measure is a mirror image of the first.

Example 125A.1.

The Bossa Nova Clave Beat

Although endless variations are possible, if you conform to the basic outlines of the clave, your music will sound more authentically Brazilian. For example, the following rhythm pattern works for most bossa nova because it does outline the clave beat.

Example 125A.2.

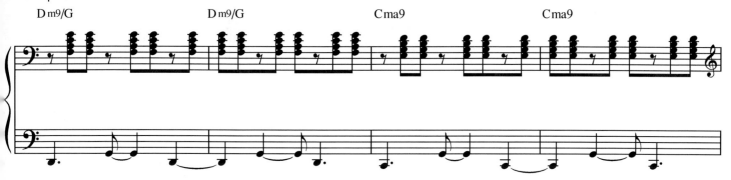

Notice how the left-hand rhythm is based on the clave beat.

Here's an eight measure phrase that uses Brazilian rhythms and very sophisticated chords. After you get the feel of it, make up some variations on this fragment or on a favorite bossa nova such as *Wave or The Girl from Ipanema*.

Example 125A.3.

Track 22

The Girl from Rio

127

New Age Piano

New age piano is expressive, impressionistic, and abstract. Rather than featuring specific melodic figures, it establishes a set of moods by using repetitive figures combined with improvisational techniques. George Winston was one of its earliest practitioners, and the nature of the music can be understood from his emphasis on various aspects of nature. He recorded a set of four albums that were designed to express the seasons of the year.

Since Winston's early example a number of other pianists like Liz Story and Peter Kater have gone on to work in a similar vein. Another group of composers like Suzanne Ciani and Ray Lynch have applied the techniques to electronic keyboards.

Often the left hand repeats a simple figure while the right hand improvises over it. Try the left hand figure below and keep playing it till it becomes automatic:

Track 23

Brand New

Next, play a right-hand figure together with it.

Our next variation adds single notes to the right hand.

Our final example keeps the left-hand figure going and adds figures in the right hand that are a bit more complex, 8th notes, rests, and a few syncopations.

Final Variations

A series of thirds brings the piece to an ambiguous conclusion.

Experiment on your own by creating left-hand figures and then improvising over them with the right hand. As you develop facility in this style you'll be able to modify the left-hand figures from time and your two hands will develop the ability to play figures where the rhythms weave in and out of the set patterns.

Piano Instruction Books

"Mikrokosmos"
By Béla Bartók. A seven volume series that will open up your technique by enabling you to achieve independence between the hands and to play in odd meters. Even if you've played for a while you may want to start with Book 1. because this is not your grandmother's piano method! Published by Boosey and Hawkes.

Blues
Aaron Blumenfeld "The Art of Blues and Barrelhouse Piano" P/F Pub. Co.

David Cohen "A Hands on Course in Traditional Blues Piano" Homespun Tapes (book & audio tape)

Eric Kriss "Six Blues-Root Pianists" Oak Pub.

Eric Kriss "Barrelhouse and Boogie Piano" (with CD) Oak Pub.

No author listed "Gotta Right to Play the Blues" a collection by various blues pianists Pearl Music

Ron Payne "Basic Blues for Piano" Hal Leonard Pub.

Country and Western
Mark Harrison "Country Piano" (with CD) Hal Leonard Pub.

New Age
"Narada New Age Piano Sampler" Hal Leonard Pub.

New Orleans
"Dr. John Teaches New Orleans Piano" Homespun Tapes (video)

Ragtime
David Cohen Homespun Tapes (Book and Cassette)

Scott Joplin "Complete Rags for Piano" Schirmer

Rock
Scott Miller "Rock Keyboard" Hal Leonard (with CD)

Andy Vitner "Rock and Roll Piano" Music Sales Pub.

Jeffrey Gutcheon "Improvising Rock Piano" Music Sales Pub.

Jeffrey Gutcheon "Teach Yourself Rock Piano" Amsco Music Pub.

Gary Turner "Rock Piano" Book & CD ADG Productions

Albums

Blues

Boogie Woogie Blues Biograph

Many recordings by Leroy Carr, Walter Davis, Champion Jack Dupree, Meade Lux Lewis.
Little Brother Montgomery, Roosevelt Sykes

Piano Blues, Vol. 1 and 2 Document

Jimmy Yancey "Chicago Piano" Atlantic

Country

Many Floyd Cramer recordings. Look for recordings where Harold "Pig" Robins and
Matt Rollings are sidemen, especially Rollings' work with Mary Chapin Carpenter

Gospel

Recordings of Thomas A. Dorsey, Mildred Falls' work with Mahalia Jackson

New Age

Look for the many recordings of Suzanne Ciani, Peter Kater, Ray Lynch, and
George Winston

Ragtime

Scott Joplin "King of the Ragtime Writers" Biograph

Piano rags by Scott Joplin (recorded by Joshua Rifkin)

Joseph Lamb Smithsonian Folkways

Rock

Look for the many recordings of Fats Domino, Billy Joel, Elton John, Johnnie Johnson (long-time pianist with Chuck Berry) and Jerry Lee Lewis

Dick Weissman

Dick Weissman is the author or co-author of 15 published books about music and the music business. The Folk Music Sourcebook, co-authored with Larry Sandberg, won the ASCAP Music Critics Award, and his recent book, Which Side Are You On? An Inside History of the Folk Music Revival in America, was a finalist for the 2006 Oregon Book Award in non-fiction writing. His other books include the Music Business; Career Opportunities & Self Defense (which was also translated into Japanese), Three Rivers Press, 3rd revised edition, 2003, a best seller on the Random House back list, Blues: the Basics, and Making A Living in your Local Music Market, 3rd revised edition, 2006. He has also written over 45 published instructional manuals for banjo, guitar, and songwriting.

While living in Colorado he was an Associate Professor in the Music & Entertainment Industry Program at the University of Colorado at Denver. He currently resides in Portland, Oregon, and is adjunct instructor at the University of Oregon, the University of Colorado at Denver and Portland Community College.

Dick has enjoyed a long career as a studio musician, record producer, songwriter, composer and performer. During the 1960s, he recorded for Capitol records in the pop-folk group The Journeymen. His 2005 album, "Solo," is an exploration of the banjo and guitar in a variety of unusual contexts that he likes to call folk jazz.

For more information about Dick Weissman, or to listen to some of his music, go to his web site: www.dickweissman.com

Dan Fox

It's likely that Dan Fox has written and sold more popular music books than any other author in recent times. His Reader's Digest songbooks (17 in all) have sold more than 10 million copies. The total approaches 20 million when you include his best-selling John Denver Songbook and Complete Beatles (in collaboration with Milt Okun), as well as songbooks for Billy Joel, Kenny Rogers; Crosby, Stills, Nash, and Young; Peter Paul and Mary; and dozens of other stars of rock, folk, and country.

Dan has also written many instruction books for guitar and mandolin, as well as "Write it Right," a guide for music arrangers and copyists, "The Rhythm Bible," with more than 1000 exercises for rock and jazz musicians; and many more. He has published arrangements and original compositions ranging from simple harmonica solos to complete works for concert bands.

Dan has published arrangements for such world-class musicians as Sir James Galway (flute), Richard Stoltzman (clarinet), and legendary tenor Luciano Pavarotti.

Dan's publishers include Mel Bay, Warner Bros. Music (where he was once editor-in-chief), Hal Leonard, Carl Fischer (where he was interim editor), Theodore Presser, and Alfred Publishing Co. He has also published "In and Out the Window" and "A Treasury of Children's Songs," highly successful children's songbooks for New York's prestigious Metropolitan Museum of Art.

Dan holds bachelor's and master's degrees in composition from the Manhattan School of Music where he was a scholarship student. He is married to artist June Fox. They have three children and seven grandchildren and divide their time between the west coast of Florida and the mountains of western North Carolina.